Battleground:

TEWKE

Eclipse of the House of Lancaster 1471

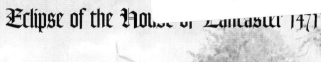

Battleground series:

Battleground: Wars of the Roses

TEWKESBURY

Eclipse of the House of Lancaster 1471

STEVEN GOODCHILD

Pen & Sword
MILITARY

To the memory of Mark Iwanczuk, who would have written a better book than me.

First published in Great Britain in 2005
and reprinted in 2014 and 2019 by
Pen and Sword Military
An imprint of
Pen & Sword Books Limited
Yorkshire - Philadelphia

ISBN 978 1 84415 190 5

A CIP catalogue record for this book is available from the British Library

Typeset in Century Old Style

Printed and bound in the UK 4edge Ltd, Essex, SS5 4AD

Pen & Sword Books Limited incorporates the imprints of Atlas,
Archaeology, Aviation, Discovery, Family History, Fiction, History, Maritime,
Military, Military Classics, Politics, Select, Transport, True Crime, Air World,
Frontline Publishing, Leo Cooper, Remember When, Seaforth Publishing,
The Praetorian Press, Wharncliffe Local History, Wharncliffe Transport,
Wharncliffe True Crime and White Owl.

For a complete list of Pen & Sword titles please contact
PEN & SWORD BOOKS LIMITED
47 Church Street, Barnsley, South Yorkshire S70 2AS, United Kingdom
E-mail: enquiries@pen-and-sword.co.uk
Website: www.pen-and-sword.co.uk
Or
PEN AND SWORD BOOKS
1950 Lawrence Rd, Havertown, PA 19083, USA
E-mail: Uspen-and-sword@casematepublishers.com
Website: www.penandswordbooks.com

Graham Turner's painting of the Battle of Tewkesbury, a detail from which is
reproduced on the cover (the complete image can be seen in the centre spread of the
colour plates) is available as a fine art print, forming part of a range of prints and cards
published from Graham Turner's historical art. A free colour catalogue is available from
Studio 88 Ltd, PO Box 568, Aylesbury, Bucks, HP17 8ZX, phone and fax
01296338504, or visit www.studio88.co.uk for details of of the full range of Graham's
original paintings.

Contents

Introduction
WAR AND THE YORKIST ASCENDANCY
1377 TO 1470

IN 1377, RICHARD, the son of the Black Prince, inherited the throne of England from his grandfather. At nine years of age, he was crowned King Richard II. He was faced with the aftermath of the Black Death and the social disruption it brought. His

confrontation of the peasants' revolt at Smithfield showed that he had some of the spirit of his grandfather, but vanity was his weakness. Thomas Walsingham describes his court as 'more devoted to Venus than to Mars, more valiant in the bedroom than the field'. His overthrow and murder by his cousin Henry Bolingbroke, Duke of Lancaster, who became King Henry IV, was a direct outcome of that weakness, and marked the beginning of the Lancastrian dynasty.

Richard II

Victory then defeat in France and the premature death of Henry V, a strong king in the Plantagenet mould, accelerated the spiral into weak government, unrestrained self-interest among the nobility and social breakdown. This escalated into the power struggle which became known as the Wars of the Roses.

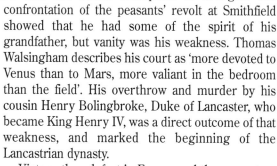

Henry IV

Henry VI was less than a year old when he became king. He was the first, and only, king to be crowned both in England and in France, though his coronation was to be his only visit to France. His reign was marked by a decline in England's fortunes, especially in France. There were those among Henry's close advisors who counselled peace and withdrawal. This view was strongly opposed by those who had made their fortunes through ravaging the French countryside. The position was complicated by the French resurgence, which made disengagement and withdrawal look like defeat and retreat.

Henry V

A weak king with unpopular policies will inevitably attract opposition. In Henry's case the

Henry VI

Queen Margaret as perceived by a Victorian artist and based upon the Tournai tapestry, Coventry (inset).

nobility also remembered that his grandfather had usurped Richard II's throne, which further undermined his authority. His cousin Richard, Duke of York, was closer in line to Edward III, through descent from his second son, Lionel, Duke of Clarence. This inheritance made him the natural focus of opposition. Richard was Henry's presumptive heir, in the absence of a son. He was prepared to tolerate this position, though considerably frustrated that the king was firmly in the hands of the peace party, whom he believed to be misguided and incompetent, and that his own counsel was ignored. This clash of interests eventually led to open warfare.

Henry VI's wife, Margaret of Anjou, had an uncanny ability to cause discontent. Margaret was the daughter of the penniless Duke

René of Anjou, and came to England without a dowry. Margaret was fiercely loyal to her friends and bore strong grudges against her enemies, and she was strongly opposed to the Duke of York's party. Within months of Henry's marriage to Margaret, the news that he had secretly ceded all English claims to Maine aroused fierce opposition, and demands that heads should roll. The stage was set for the wars.

As if the situation was not already complicated enough, King Henry suffered from bouts of insanity, a condition he is said to have inherited from his grandfather, the French King Charles VI, through his mother, Catherine of Valois. In August 1453, at the height of a wave of discontent, with the Nevilles and the Percys fighting private battles in the north, he lost his reason. He was to remain in this state for sixteen months. Parliament declared Richard of York Protector of the Realm. At that point such recognition was probably the height of his ambition.

Two months later, on 13 October, Margaret bore a son, Edward. When Henry recovered his wits, he acknowledged this boy as his heir. At a stroke, York's hopes of inheritance were shattered, and it may be that from this point the struggle shifted from one for control of the king to one for the crown itself.

Fighting started in earnest with the first battle of St Albans in 1455. This was not on the scale of the later battles, and the Yorkist party was content with the death there of Edmund Beaufort, Duke of Somerset, the last of King Henry's reviled advisors. Henry was captured and forced to accept a government led by the Yorkist party. Richard of York was again appointed Protector. Richard, Earl of Warwick, the son of his closest supporter, the Earl of Salisbury, was appointed Captain of Calais. The strategic importance of Calais was that it was the base for the only standing army the realm possessed, and Warwick, best known to history as the 'Kingmaker', was to have a very long and fruitful association with this city.

Now that King Henry's most powerful advisors had been removed, the impetus for the Lancastrian struggle came from Queen Margaret, who managed to regain control of the government, but not of Calais, which became the focus for the growing discontent of the Yorkists.

Henry was recaptured by the Yorkists at the Battle of Northampton in July 1460, and again became a puppet for a Yorkist government. York now made a badly misjudged claim for the throne, which was rejected by an uneasy Parliament. The country was in ferment. Margaret had no difficulty in raising a large army, in opposition to the Yorkist protectorate, and overran large parts of the realm. Battle was fully joined at Wakefield on 30 December, and the Yorkist party were thoroughly defeated. Richard, Duke of York was amongst the slain. The Neville Earl of Salisbury was taken alive and beheaded by the Percys. The heads of these men, with the head of York's youngest son Edmund, who was also killed in the battle, were displayed above Micklegate Bar in York. A paper crown decorated the Duke of York's head.

For the Yorkists, defeat and the death of their elder statesmen brought the next generation of leaders into the spotlight. It was these men who grasped the moment – and the throne. York's son Edward assumed his title and his ambition. Salisbury's son

Edward IV

Warwick, the Kingmaker, encouraged him in this adventure.

Margaret's army moved towards London, but was allowed to pillage the land as it went, putting such fear into the City that it refused entry. Edward of York met and defeated Lancastrian reinforcements recruited by the Earl of Pembroke at the battle of Mortimer's Cross. Warwick met the queen's army at St Albans and was defeated. London was panic-stricken but resolute. Margaret's army began to desert, and victory became bitter defeat. The Lancastrians withdrew to the north. York and Warwick were welcomed into London, and on 4 March Edward of York was declared king by the merchants and commoners of London.

On 29 March 1461, Palm Sunday, the two sides met again, this time on the wide plain at Towton in Yorkshire. The battle was fought in a blizzard, which severely disadvantaged the Lancastrians, who were comprehensively defeated. They were finished as a credible ruling party. From this date Edward IV was the undisputed king of England. The Lancastrians retreated further north to continue their struggle, almost guerrilla-style, among the castles of the Scottish marches.

Margaret appealed to Scotland and France, but Edward countered this attempt to 'internationalise' the struggle by negotiating truces with both countries. Warwick's brother John, Lord Montague, defeated Lancastrian forces at Hedgeley Moor and Hexham. The Lancastrians retreated into Northumbrian castles. They were besieged and fell to the Yorkists. Margaret left for France with her son. King Henry had been separated from his wife, and for a while wandered the North. He was captured in 1465 by the cousins Thomas and John Talbot at a house of religion at Clitheroe in Lancashire, betrayed by a Black Monk of Abingdon and was taken to the Tower.

Warwick saw himself as a statesman and diplomat playing on the European stage. He had carefully cultivated a relationship with the new king of France, Louis XI (or more likely Louis had cultivated him, and drawn him, unwittingly, into his web of intrigue). He also believed that his power over Edward would be of the same order as that which Henry's advisors had exercised. This was not to be. Whilst Warwick was negotiating for a French wife for his king, Edward rushed headlong into a marriage with an Englishwoman (at a time when English kings almost never married into English families) which seemed to be based on little more than lust. In her own way this queen, Elizabeth Woodville, caused as many problems for England as Margaret of Anjou had done. She came with a large family, who were given unashamed preferment in the realm, displacing Warwick from his position as the king's confidant and advisor.

Warwick's preferred foreign policy, for which he had done considerable groundwork, was an alliance with France. Such an alliance would immediately damage relations with Burgundy, which included the rich Flanders provinces that were England's trading partners in the extremely lucrative wool trade. Warwick was against the proposed marriage between Charles, heir to the Duke of Burgundy, and Margaret of York, King Edward's sister. Whilst Warwick was in France negotiating a treaty, this marriage was arranged by Queen Elizabeth's brother. By the time the ceremony took place, the old Duke of Burgundy was dead, and Charles, known to the English as Charles the Bold, had inherited what was possibly

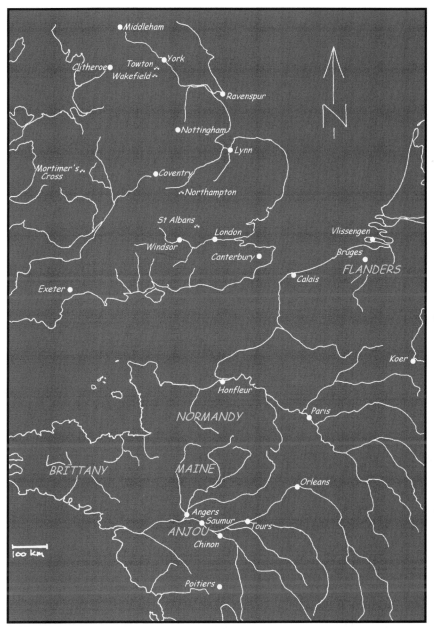

Map of England and France in the Wars of the Roses. Though the battles, known as the Wars of the Roses, were in England, the causes can be traced back to French aspirations.

11

Middleham Castle. Warwick the Kingmaker's power base in North Yorkshire.
Richard III Foundation

the richest and grandest court in Europe.

King Edward's not very subtle policy of snubbing him and preferring the queen's avaricious relatives drove Warwick out of court. He retired in disgust to his castle at Middleham, in Yorkshire, and began to plot against the king. Edward's rule was insecure. There were civil disturbances and food shortages in the land and sections of the nobility were alienated by the favour shown to the Woodvilles. To make matters worse, Edward's French policy was anything but conciliatory and a plan to go to war with France to recover English territories lost during the reign of Henry VI was being considered.

Warwick cultivated the king's brother, George, Duke of Clarence. A teenager and easily led, George was converted to rebellion. He was to be the puppet through whom Warwick would again rule. Warwick's first move was to betroth the duke to his eldest daughter Isabel. Though King Edward was clearly opposed, even to the extent of petitioning the Pope against the wedding, it took place in Calais on 11 July 1469, the ceremony being conducted by Warwick's brother George, Archbishop of York.

Meanwhile, unrest in the North, probably stirred up by Warwick, was turning into rebellion. The focus became 'Robin of Redesdale', a mysterious figure unidentified to this day. The rebels grouped in Lancashire to march to London and present their grievances to the king. Robin's manifesto accused the king of alienating the peerage, and of living beyond his means at the expense of his subjects.

Parallels were drawn with the conditions that led to the overthrow of some of the king's predecessors, which should have given Edward cause to reflect on his position.

At first King Edward did not take this insurrection seriously, and made his way north at a leisurely pace. In Nottingham, his position became perilous. On 12 July, Warwick, who had returned from Calais with his new son-in-law, issued a manifesto with a close similarity to that of Robin of Redesdale. At Canterbury he met fellow rebels and they marched to join the northern army. He had shown his hand. King Edward's situation was made worse when his two commanders, the Earls of Pembroke and Devon, were confronted by the rebels at the attle of Edgecote on 26 July and defeated. The Earl of Pembroke and his brother Sir Richard Herbert were captured and executed, without trial, on the orders of Warwick, who arrived on the scene soon after the battle.

King Edward suddenly found himself alone, without an army to defend him. He surrendered himself to Warwick, who immediately engaged in a purge of royal advisors. Queen Elizabeth's father, Lord

An artist's impression of Warwick the Kingmaker, as lord of Glamorgan and Mogannwg, part of his Beauchamp inheritance.

Rivers, and brother, Sir John Woodville, were captured and executed. Warwick seemed to have gained the power which he craved.

King Edward was secured in Middleham Castle while Warwick set about the business of legalising his new position. But the unrest grew among Lancastrian sympathisers, and there were stirrings of support for the other captive king, Henry VI, incarcerated in the Tower of London. Warwick's name was not sufficient to raise troops to counter this new threat, and he was forced to give King Edward his freedom as a focus for the army. The rebellion was crushed, the leaders executed, but the king was free. Ironically, the executed leaders, Sir Humphrey Neville and his brother Charles, were Warwick's cousins.

13

The ensuing peace must have been an uneasy one. King Edward granted a general pardon, but he would have neither forgotten nor forgiven the murder of his father-in-law and brother-in-law. His wife would have ensured that.

Presumably because his bid to be the power behind the throne had come to nothing, and had created such tension between himself and the king, Warwick continued to plot. A few months later, in February 1470, a local difficulty between two Lincolnshire landowners was elevated to the status of a rebellion against the crown by Warwick's subtle interventions and encouragement. The rebellion was led by Sir Robert Welles. King Edward moved to confront him and his followers. If Edward was aware of Warwick's and Clarence's part in the proceedings, he did not let it affect his outward attitude towards them. The rebels were crushed by the king at the battle of Empingham, better known as Losecote Field because of the speed with which the fleeing rebels threw off their liveries in their haste to escape. Their battle cries, 'A Warwick' and 'A Clarence' must have given Edward cause to doubt their loyalty, and more damning proof of their involvement was obtained from the prisoners. Welles was captured, and confessed all. King Edward now commanded Warwick and Clarence to appear before him 'in humble wise', to answer grave charges against them.

Warwick and Clarence toured the North looking for support, which was not forthcoming. Indeed, Warwick's soldiers were beginning to understand that their fate was likely to be a traitor's noose, and were deserting him in numbers. King Edward issued more and more terse demands for their surrender. The fugitives made their way to Exeter, and from there to Dartmouth, where they took ship with Warwick's wife and daughters. Their destination was Calais, where Warwick was Captain. Calais, though, had been ordered by King Edward not to admit them, and there was nothing that Lord Wenlock, Warwick's man in the city, could do to assist, save send a little wine, and advise that they go to France. Warwick anchored his fleet off Honfleur, on the Seine. The Duke of Burgundy protested strongly to the French King Louis that harbouring Warwick, who had been attacking Burgundian merchant ships, was a contravention of the truce just agreed between them. This was not a very auspicious arrival, and Warwick must have wondered where his adventure was leading him.

Chapter One

THE SHORT RESTORATION OF HENRY VI
1470 to 1471

ON 22 JULY 1470, Richard Neville, Earl of Warwick, the Kingmaker, met Margaret of Anjou, Queen of England, in Angers to make his peace with her. They reached an agreement about the re-conquest of England. This unlikely alliance was the culmination of some extremely patient Gallic diplomacy on the part of Louis XI of France. Margaret hated Warwick. She blamed him for all the ills which had befallen her in the years she had been Queen of England, and particularly for his role in her husband Henry VI's, overthrow and the accession of the Yorkist Edward IV.

The Milanese Ambassador, Sforza de Bettini, reported from Angers to the Duke of Milan:

'The Queen of England and the Prince of Wales, her son, arrived here the day before yesterday, and on the same day the Earl of Warwick also arrived. The same evening the king presented him to the queen. With great reverence Warwick went on his knees and asked her pardon for the injuries and

Angers Castle in France, scene of the 'reconciliation' between Warwick and the Lancastrian ex-queen Margaret. Following this they joined forces and plotted to overthrow Yorkist King Edward IV.

wrongs done to her in the past. She graciously forgave him and he afterwards did homage and fealty there, swearing to be a faithful and loyal subject of the king, queen, and prince as his liege lords unto his death.'

Some say that Margaret kept Warwick on his knees for a considerable time. She was very bitter, and would not easily forgive the injuries and wrongs.

Louis cared little about Margaret. His whole purpose was to consolidate France as a nation, building on his father's work to repair the damage done by the English invasions. Though Warwick was an old and admired friend, he did not hesitate to use him as part of the web he had woven around Europe to further his, and French, interests. He knew that Warwick had been involved in an attempt to overthrow Edward and put his brother George, Duke of Clarence, on the throne. This had gone badly wrong and the two had slipped out of the country. Being warned of an ambush in English Calais, they had moved on, eventually landing at Honfleur. They were not in a strong bargaining position, and they would become enmeshed in Louis' plan to subdue his cousin Charles, Duke of Burgundy.

Fat, ugly, paranoid and ruthless, King Louis XI, 'the universal spider', single-mindedly rebuilt France after the Hundred Years War.

The Hundred Years War had played havoc with the French nation. English greed had created an anarchy which took many years to repair. First the Dauphin, Charles VII, and then his son Louis XI led the recovery of the nation, which was very successful in removing English authority, but it left 'free companies', mercenary soldiers willing to hire themselves for any cause, and quite able to create havoc of their own. It also left dukes with a taste for independence, who had to be brought back to fealty. Chief among these was the Duke of Burgundy, the king's cousin, who held a swathe of land north-east of France, stretching from Flanders to Alsace, and who presided over the most opulent court in Europe.

Queen Margaret had been languishing

in the country since her flight, ill-regarded by Louis, who probably saw her as an embarrassment. His policy was entirely dedicated to subjugating the French duchies, and he had no desire to become embroiled in England. He was happy to maintain a peace with the Yorkist king. Margaret was not well provided for in France. Duke René, her father, had involved himself in feckless adventures which had left him virtually bankrupt. She was seldom at the court of Louis, living with her son and small entourage of exiled Lancastrians at Koeur castle, in Lorraine. Sir John Fortescue, Lancastrian Chancellor and tutor to the Prince of Wales, wrote 'we are all in great poverty' but since 'the queen sustains us in meat and drink, we are not in extreme necessity'.

Warwick was a pirate as well as a politician. After his flight from England his ships had been warned not to enter Calais, and had spent some time in preying on Hanseatic and Burgundian shipping, before being obliged to enter the Seine by the presence of the English fleet, under the command of Lord Howard. His intention was probably simple self-preservation, but it caused some difficulty to King Louis, who was conscious that harbouring ships which had attacked the Burgundians was a contravention of his truce with Duke Charles, who demanded the arrest of the pirates.

The outcome of Louis' efforts was a plan to recover England for the Lancastrians, sealed by a contract of marriage between Edward, Prince of Wales, and Anne, Warwick's youngest daughter (his eldest daughter having been married to the Duke of Clarence to cement the earlier alliance). In return for his support, Louis had been promised that as soon as Lancastrian rule again prevailed in England, war would be declared against Burgundy.

When his daughter's betrothal was solemnised, on 25 July at Angers Cathedral, Warwick sailed for England with an army. Margaret stayed in France with her court, because she still did not trust Warwick. Louis was happy with this arrangement, seeing her as a hostage against Warwick fulfilling his obligation to declare war on Burgundy. This caution of Louis' led to long delays in her return, and possibly to the failure of the cause. French matters went well for Louis, though. He had other irons in the fire.

Warwick's fleet slipped from harbour when the blockading English were scattered by a storm. His army landed unopposed in Devon in September 1470. He was accompanied by some of Margaret's exiled Lancastrians, among whom were John de Vere, Earl of Oxford, and Jasper Tudor, Earl of Pembroke, as well as

George, Duke of Clarence, who surely had not anticipated this when he first plotted with Warwick. They issued a joint proclamation declaring their commitment to King Henry, condemning Edward as a traitor and usurper. People flocked to the cause, and the Lancastrian army gained great strength as it progressed towards London, where it arrived early in October. King Henry was released from the Tower and restored to the throne.

King Edward was in the North to put down a rebellion led by Henry, Lord FitzHugh, Warwick's brother-in-law. Returning south, he was again wrong-footed by the defection of the Marquis Montague, Warwick's brother, to the Lancastrian cause. He was suddenly placed in a perilous situation. Without the strength to fight, he left the country to seek refuge with his own brother-in-law, the Duke of Burgundy.

The Coventry Leet Book describes the events succinctly:

'And in the month of September the said duke and the earl with the Earl of Oxford, the Earl of Pembroke, brother to King Harry, Bastard of Fauconberg landed at Exmouth. There they drew to them many people. Before they came to Coventry there were 30,000. King Edward lay at Nottingham and sent for lords and other men, but there came so few people to him that he was unable to make a field against them. Then he, with Earl Rivers, Lord Hastings, Lord Howard and Lord Say went to Lynn, and there obtained ships and sailed to the Duke of Burgundy, who had married King Edward's sister, the Lady Margaret. And then the Duke of Clarence, the Earl of Warwick, the Earl of Oxford, the Earl of Shrewsbury, Lord Stanley and the archbishop went to the Tower of London and released King Henry VI from prison, who had been nine and a half [years] and more a prisoner, brought him to the bishop's palace at St Paul's, and made him king again.'

King Henry was, by all accounts, a sad and bewildered figure. It was said that he had been mistreated in captivity, but there are also hints about his mental competence. He had probably never completely recovered from his breakdown in 1453. This was the sort of puppet the Earl of Warwick wanted, though he would have been well aware that Queen Margaret would have had her own agenda.

Warwick's government of England was doomed by the promise he had made to King Louis. Queen Margaret and Prince Edward remained in France, their departure for England being delayed until King Louis had confirmation that England had declared for France, and against Burgundy. Although without this commitment Warwick's adventure would not have been possible, it unleashed the powers which brought about his downfall.

The London merchants, whose wealth was dependant on trade with Flanders, reacted badly. They would not provide the loans which Warwick needed to pursue the war, or even to govern the country. The Lancastrian nobility was also upset. They had sought an alliance with Duke Charles, to isolate Edward. The most serious reaction, though, came from Duke Charles himself. Far from being an automatic supporter of Edward he had seen his presence as a refugee in Flanders as a nuisance. Now, though, he was prepared to sponsor Edward's return to England, to overthrow Warwick's new government. England had become a pawn in Louis' struggle to unite the French kingdom.

Charles the Bold, Duke of Burgundy.

In March 1471 King Edward left Vlissingen, on the River Schelde estuary, with a fleet of thirty-six ships and over 1,000 men. Warkworth's Chronicle says there were 900 Englishmen and 300 Flemings with hand guns. Warwick had seen to it that Lancastrian sympathisers in the north and east were reinforced, and that any landfall would be hostile to Yorkists. Edward discovered this when he eventually landed at Ravenspur, on the north

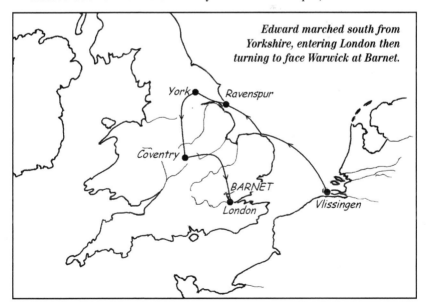

Edward marched south from Yorkshire, entering London then turning to face Warwick at Barnet.

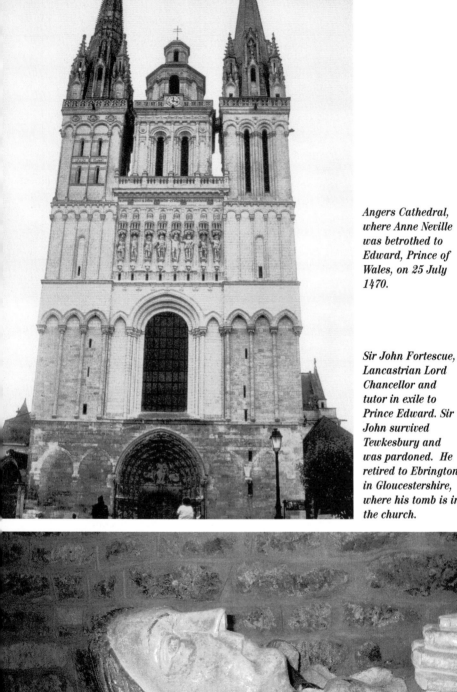

Angers Cathedral, where Anne Neville was betrothed to Edward, Prince of Wales, on 25 July 1470.

Sir John Fortescue, Lancastrian Lord Chancellor and tutor in exile to Prince Edward. Sir John survived Tewkesbury and was pardoned. He retired to Ebrington in Gloucestershire, where his tomb is in the church.

coast of the Humber estuary, after a stormy and uncomfortable voyage. He said that he had returned to reclaim his Yorkist inheritance, and not the crown. (This ruse had also been used by Henry Bolingbroke when he returned from exile, also landing at Ravenspur, to overthrow King Richard II and establish the Lancastrian dynasty.) As proof of his loyalty, he wore the ostrich feather badge of the Prince of Wales. This gained him a foothold and some time. He survived a tense and dangerous visit to York and proceeded southwards with his little army. Though the Earl of Northumberland, Lord Montague and the Earl of Oxford all had armies in the area, no one opposed him though no one joined him, until he reached the Midlands, where Lord Hastings' household provided 3,000 men, and other smaller contingents rallied to his cause. He then revealed his true intention.

Always a competent commander, King Edward was at his most inspired in this campaign. He moved quickly to confront Warwick at Coventry, before the Lancastrian forces could unite. Not only was Warwick too weak to risk a battle, but he was also weakened further by the defection of Clarence. Always looking to his personal interests, Clarence must have re-evaluated his position, and decided that he had no future with the Warwick/Lancaster alliance. Edward had made secret approaches to him, and he chose his moment well to change sides again.

Warkworth's Chronicle says:

'But the Earl of Warwick had a letter from the Duke of Clarence that he should not fight with him until he came himself; and all was to the destruction of the Earl of Warwick, as it happened afterwards. Yet so the Earl of Warwick still kept the gates of the town shut, and suffered King Edward to pass towards London; and a little out of Warwick the Duke of Clarence met with King Edward, and with 7,000 men, and there they were reconciled, and made a proclamation forthwith in King Edward's name; and so all covenants of fidelity made between the Duke of Clarence and the Earl of Warwick, Queen Margaret and Prince Edward her son, both in England and in France, were clearly broken and forsaken by the said Duke of Clarence; which, in the end, brought destruction both to him and them, for perjury shall never have a good ending, without the great grace of God.'

John Warkworth clearly disapproved of such behaviour, and Shakespeare immortalised him as 'False, fleeting, perjured Clarence'.

Edward's entry into London was unopposed. He was said by

Philippe de Commines to have been supported by Yorkists coming out of sanctuary, the merchants who saw this as their only opportunity for repayment of their loans, and the persuasive powers of influential ladies with whom Edward had earlier been closely and secretly acquainted. The mayor took to his bed, the people were commanded to go home to dinner, and King Edward re-took the throne. Poor King Henry was paraded through the streets in what was supposed to be a procession to rally support, but he cut such a poor figure in his long blue gown that he became an object of ridicule. He greeted Edward warmly, saying 'My cousin of York, you are very welcome: I know that in your hands my life will not be in danger.'

Edward remained two days in London, before leaving to face the Earl of Warwick, who was approaching from the north. He took King Henry with him.

The battle of Barnet was fought on Easter Sunday, 14 April 1471. If Warwick had hoped to catch Edward unawares at Easter observances, as was reported, he must have been clutching at straws. The armies camped for the night on Barnet Common, so close together that they spent the night shooting at each other. Battle commenced in a thick early morning mist and in the confusion Warwick's army managed to turn their early advantage into defeat. Warwick's brother John Neville, Marquis Montague, was killed in the field, apparently in the act of changing sides. Warwick the Kingmaker himself fled from the field, was spotted, and cut down in a nearby wood. The Neville brothers' bodies were taken to St Paul's Cathedral, where they were left on display before being secretly buried. The Earl of Oxford fled to Scotland. King Henry was returned to his familiar lodgings in the Tower.

Chapter Two

MARGARET'S RETURN
April 1471

FOUR DAYS after the battle of Barnet, on 18 April 1471, Sir John Paston wrote to his mother Margaret:

'Mother, I recommend me to you, letting you know that, blessed be God, my brother John is alive and fares well, and in no peril of death. Nevertheless he is hurt with an arrow on his right arm beneath the elbow, and I have sent him a surgeon who has dressed him, and he tells me that he trusts that he shall be all whole within a right short time. John Mylsent is dead, God have mercy on his soul, and William Mylsent is alive and his other servants have all escaped in all likelihood.

'As for me, I am in good health, blessed be God, and in no jeopardy of my life if I take care, for I am at my liberty; if need be.

'My lord Archbishop is in the Tower. Nevertheless I trust to God that he shall do well enough. He has a safeguard for him and me both. Nevertheless we have been troubled since, but now I understand that he has a pardon, and so we hope well. There were killed upon the field half a mile from Barnet, on Easter Day, the Earle of Warwick, the Marquis Montagu, Sir William Tyrell, Sir Lowes John, and diverse other squires of our country. And in King Edward's party, the Lord Cromwell, the Lord Say, Sir Humphrey Bouchier of our country, and other people off both parties to the number off more than one thousand.

'As for other tidings it is understand here that the Queen Margaret is verily landed, and her son, in the west country; and I believe that tomorrow or else the next day the King Edward will depart from here towards her to drive her out again.

'I ask you that I may be recommended to my cousin Lomnore, and to thank him for his goodwill towards me if I had had need. And I beseech you on my behalf to warn him to be well aware of his dealings or language as yet, for the world, I assure you, is right uneasy, as you shall know within this month. The people here fear it sore. God hath shown himself marvelously, like him that made all and can undo again when he would like;

and I can think that by all likelihood shall show himself as marvelous again, and that in short time, and as I suppose oftener then once in like cases.

'It is so that my brother is without money. I have helped him to my power and above, wherefore, as it pleases you, remember him, for I can not provide for my-self in the same case.

'Written at London the Thursday in Easter Week. I hope hastily to see you. All this letter must be secret. Be ye not in despair of the world, for I trust all shall be well. If it thus continue I am not all undone, nere noon off is; and if otherwise, then, &c.'

Sir John's message speaks urgently of the plight of a Lancastrian following the Yorkist victory. He also speaks of Queen Margaret's arrival in the West Country, only four days after her landing, and offered some speculation as to Edward's response.

Margaret's departure from France had been a struggle. First she had to put up with Louis' prevarication as he waited for England to declare war on Burgundy. Then she had to endure a further forced delay in Honfleur, this time caused by the westerly spring gales which held her little fleet firmly in the River Seine. Eventually, they were able to sail, and landed on the south coast. She brought with her

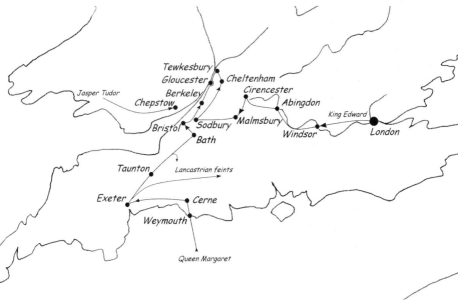

The routes to Sodbury Hill. The two armies played cat and mouse over most of south-west England before Margaret was finally cornered at Tewkesbury.

24

Edward, Prince of Wales, John, Lord Wenlock and John Beaufort, the Marquis of Dorset, brother of Edmund Beaufort, Duke of Somerset. Margaret herself landed at Weymouth. Others of her party landed as far away as Southampton, suggesting that the voyage was just as uncomfortable as that of King Edward's from Flanders.*

She was welcomed by those 'Old Lancastrians' already in England, but who had not joined Warwick in the Barnet campaign: Edmund Beaufort, Sir John Courtenay, Earl of Devonshire, Sir John Langstrother, prior of the Order of St John, Sir John Fortescue and Dr John Morton. Jasper Tudor was arraying troops in South Wales. The party stayed at Cerne Abbey. There, on Easter Monday, came the news of the disaster at Barnet.

There must have been a great deal of soul-searching. Her arrival should have been to a triumphant procession to rejoin her husband in London, but all plans had come to nought. She would have known about Edward's arrival in England more than a month earlier, and of his purpose. She would have hoped, though, to have been in time to raise an army in the west to join Warwick, and now it was too late. To return to France must have been considered as an option, but to return to penniless exile was not a very inviting choice. Her purpose was to restore her son's inheritance, and this she chose to do. Not surprisingly, when the Countess of Warwick heard the news of the death of her husband and brother-in-law she immediately chose to seek sanctuary in the Abbey at Beaulieu in the New Forest.

The Crowland Chronicler speculates that Margaret was counselled to 'pass swiftly along the western coast – perhaps through Bristol, Gloucester and Chester – to reach Lancashire, where a considerable number of archers were to be found'. This seems to have been the plan she adopted. The arraying of an army began in considerable earnest. Margaret moved to Exeter, and the whole of the West Country was whipped into ferment:

> 'And so, forthwith, they sent all about in Somerset, Dorset and part of Wiltshire, to ready and array the people by a certain day, such as the Lords and their supporters laboured greatly to that end, preparing the country by all possible means. And, so that they would gather up and array the power of Devonshire and

*The Yorkist army took with it a correspondent who recorded the progress from Flanders through England to Barnet, to Tewkesbury, and finally to the siege of London led by the Bastard of Falconberg. His account survived the centuries, and has been published with the title 'A historie of the Arrivall of Edward IV in England and the final recoverie of his kingdoms from Henry VI AD M.CCCCLXXI'. This title has been abbreviated to 'the Arrivall'.

Cornwall, they moved from thence more westwards to the City of Exeter, moving Edward, called prince, and his mother, the Queen, to do the same, trusting that showing their presence in the country would cause more people to come to their help and assistance, and sooner.' (The *Arrivall*)

The tactic was a good one. They were able to bring more men to their cause than the earlier efforts of the Earl of Warwick, because the call came from the Lords of Somerset and Devonshire, the 'old inheritors of the country'.

Meanwhile, King Edward, who had good intelligence of the activity in the west, moved with more alacrity than he had shown on campaigns a few months earlier. He had problems with his army, which had been partly disbanded, and had not had a lot of time to recover from Barnet Field. He sent for fresh men from among his supporters, and 'purveyed artilary, and ordinaunce, gonns, and other, for the field gret plentye'. The preparations were hurried, but being made from London there was better access to all the things an army needed.

Having done what he could, Edward moved his headquarters to his castle at Windsor. Here he celebrated the feast of St George, and the annual Garter ceremony, and was able to relax a little. He had nominated Windsor as the assembly point for his soldiers and all the many specialists needed to support the coming expedition. He had time to think in the days it took to assemble the forces. He reasoned that the Lancastrians had three options open to them. They could march directly on London, through the city of Salisbury. They could go along the south coast, through Hampshire, Sussex and Kent, increasing the size of their army as they marched, and so to London. The third possibility was that they would look to maximise their strength by joining with Jasper Tudor's forces and travelling north into Cheshire and Lancashire. This third was judged the most likely, as Edward was well aware of the activities of Jasper Tudor in Wales and the Lancastrian support in the North-West. Queen Margaret had looked to the Cheshire archers in a previous hour of need. He sent out his spies, who regularly reported back to him about Lancastrian sympathisers, and the activity of the main forces. If they were moving directly on London, he proposed to confront them as far from London as possible. If they were moving north, then they would be confronted in Gloucestershire. This was the campaign plan.

Queen Margaret's army took to the road, and caused as much confusion as they could. The first detachment took the road to

Shaftesbury and thence to Salisbury while the main army marched towards Taunton. From Taunton, they took the road to Wells via Glastonbury. They sent to the surrounding towns to array troops, and let it be known that they intended to travel to Reading, and then through Berkshire and Oxfordshire to London. None of this fooled King Edward. In Wells, they disgraced themselves, and presumably alienated a lot of potential support, by sacking the Bishop's palace and breaking open the prison, releasing all the prisoners.

We have an interesting glimpse of the army passing Glastonbury, because John, Lord Wenlock, decided to leave his valuables in safe keeping with the abbott. Evidence of this is in a deed drawn up for their return between Agnes, Wenlock's wife, and Abbot Selwood and dated 20 May; sixteen days after the battle of Tewkesbury. The valuables consisted of 'a cup of gold, a little salt cellar of gold, a book called a portnos and a locked casket stuffed with such jewels and other things'. The abbot received 200 marks to cover his costs. This incident also suggests that Agnes was with the army on the march, probably therefore accompanying the queen.

Meanwhile, Edward's army had moved out of Windsor after the St George's Day observance. Five days marching found him in Cirencester, where the army was billeted in the town to await developments. These came quickly.

His spies told him that the Lancastrians were approaching Bath,

The crest of Sodbury Hill is marked by a castellated Victorian ventilation shaft, from the railway tunnel far below. This is where Edward waited for the Lancastrians to come to battle.

which they were, and that they would come straight on from there to do battle. Edward moved his men out of town and he and they spent the night in a field three miles out of Cirencester. By the time they had reached Malmesbury he learned that this was another Lancastrian ruse, and the army had turned towards Bristol:

'a good and strong walled town, where they were greatly refreshed and relieved by such as were the king's rebels in that town, of money, men and artillery, where through they took new courage, the Thursday after, to take the field and give the king battle, to which intent they had sent fore-riders to a town nine miles from Bristol, called Sodbury, and, a mile towards the king, they appointed a ground for their field at a place called Sodbury Hill.'

Among the Lancastrians killed at Tewkesbury was Nicholas Hervey, recorder of Bristol. He would have been part of the contingent joining the army at that point.

Edward did not waste time. He clearly thought that they were serious this time. He advanced to Sodbury Hill. Here was first blood to the Lancastrians, when advance parties from both armies met in Sodbury town; the Yorkists seeking out lodgings, the Lancastrians intent on convincing Edward that a whole army was following them. The *Arrivall* says that 'they distressed certain of the king's party, five or six, such as negligently pressed so far forward, dreading no danger...'. The deception seemed to be working, and Edward had no clear idea of the Lancastrian movements. He did not know if they intended to fight, or even if they were close. He was cautious and camped there overnight. Meanwhile, Queen Margaret had taken her army in quite another direction. They marched all night, across the vale towards Berkeley.

Chipping Sodbury where armed men clashed in the streets.

Chapter Three

BRISTOL TO TEWKESBURY
Thursday and Friday, 2 and 3 May, 1471

THE LANCASTRIAN ARMY had no intention of facing the Yorkists. The Yorkist army had more or less reached its full strength and was ready for battle, while the Lancastrians needed to grow both in size and experience. Although they were in Lancastrian territory, their advantage would only come with time, which Margaret was desperate to gain. The forces arrayed by Jasper Tudor, Earl of Pembroke were approaching to join them, just on the other side of the Bristol Channel, and they had many supporters further north. The army was large, but many of the men had been taken from the villages of the West Country and were embarking on a totally unfamiliar adventure. They desperately needed the experience of these senior Lancastrian lords and their troops.

All their tactics had been to gain time to grow stronger but now time was becoming a precious commodity. Although the detour to Bristol had gained them a lot, in men, equipment and the morale-raising knowledge that one of England's major cities was with them, it had cost them their lead in the race. From now on they would have to pass rapidly through the land, and recruiting would not be a priority.

Margaret must have been surprised and relieved that Edward had been taken in by the Sodbury feint. His army was in a position to intercept but his spies inexplicably seemed to have failed him in a country where it is possible to see long distances. Those hours while Edward made camp were very precious, as the Lancastrian force marched towards Berkeley. Edward's tactic may have been a deliberate one. If Margaret was not in the vicinity of Sodbury, her army could have been moving only in one direction – to the north. She was moving into an angle of the land from which the only ways out were to cross the Severn, or to change direction and move east over the Cotswold escarpment. He was well positioned to shepherd her along the river by shadowing her and maintaining a position slightly south and east which would allow him to react quickly if her army showed signs of moving off the planned track.

Edward got news of the direction Margaret had taken at three

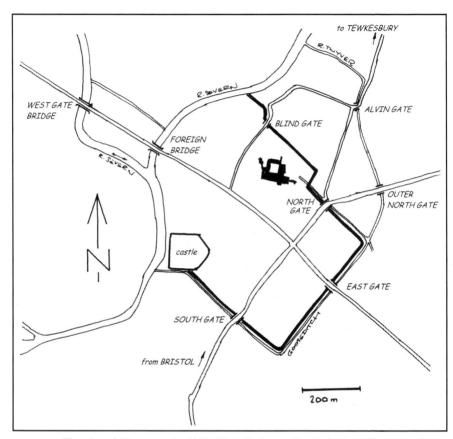

The city of Gloucester in 1471. Though the medieval city has disappeared and one arm of the River Severn has disappeared, the road plan and line of the walls can still be traced.

o'clock in the morning on Friday 3 May: 'The King had certain tidings that they had taken their way by Berkeley toward Gloucester'. This was the news he undoubtedly expected. He called a council of his advisors, presumably simply to confirm what he had long decided to do. Riders were despatched to Gloucester with messages for the governor of the castle. The army was roused and prepared for the road.

'The King, the same morning, the Friday, early, advanced his banners and divided his whole host in three battles, and sent before him his fore-riders and scourers, on every side him, and so, in fair array, and ordinance, he took his way through the champion country, called Cotswold, travelling all his people,

30

whereof were more than three thousand footmen, that Friday,
which was right-an-hot day, thirty miles and more.'

The armies were now moving towards the end game.

The fifteenth-century roads of England were not straight and smooth. They had grown from necessity and were often seasonal, serving the needs of itinerant people and animal drovers. The routes with the clearest definition were those left by the Romans and those connecting major towns and cities. Margaret was travelling in the Severn vale, a fertile land full of villages and agriculture. Having convinced Edward's spies that she was marching towards Chipping Sodbury, she turned north, towards Gloucester, where she hoped to enter the gates of Gloucester and there either await the coming of Jasper Tudor or pass over the Severn to meet him in the Forest of Dean. Her route would have been straightforward, following the roads from Bristol, unless she had indeed taken her army along the road towards Sodbury, in which case the road to Berkeley would have been complicated, uncomfortably close to the Cotswold escarpment, and somewhat out of the way if the objective was to get to Gloucester. It seems much more likely that she relied on a significant body of fore-riders to deceive the Yorkists, whilst the main force marched along the direct route to Berkeley, through Thornbury and then to the west of the present A38. The timings of

The Champion Country. The open wolds above Sodbury; the route of the Yorkist march.

orkist line of
advance

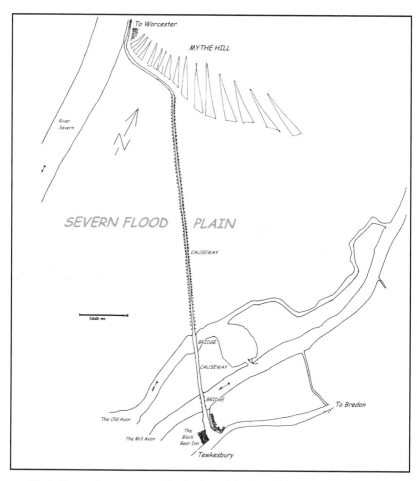

The bridge and causeway at Tewkesbury. The Long Bridge crossed the River Avon and the flood plain with two bridges and two causeways.

this march are not given to us very precisely. The distance covered is about twenty-four miles, which is a good day's march for an army, the majority being on foot and manoeuvring the ordnance and supplies in wagons over surfaces which were hardly purpose-built for the process.

Though Berkeley is named as a destination in the *Arrivall*, it would be a strange choice of resting place, as the Berkeley family, custodians of the castle, were staunchly Yorkist. Sir William, Lord Berkeley, was the Yorkist Commissioner of Array for Gloucestershire. His brother Maurice was a personal retainer of

The Mythe Hill and causeway. The causeway across the flood plain to the safety of the Mythe Hill was built up on wooden piles in the fifteenth century.

William, Lord Hastings, Edward's chamberlain, and was to be knighted at Tewkesbury. Even if both were away from the castle, the garrison was hardly likely to welcome a Lancastrian army into the town. Given the distances, and the evidence from the *Arrivall* that the army marched through the night (which must have been a desperate measure given the state of the roads and the lack of any reliable lighting), it does not seem likely that they had any rest at all. The twenty-four miles to Berkeley were immediately followed by a further fourteen to Gloucester, where they arrived at about ten in the morning. These thirty-eight miles were travelled in little more than twenty-four hours, with no respite, no pre-planning and provisioning, no logistical support, and an overriding need for caution. In all the circumstances, the march seems little short of miraculous.

There is a local legend that Queen Margaret spent the night of Thursday 2 to Friday 3 May in Owlpen Manor, which is tucked into a fold of the Cotswold escarpment beyond Dursley, below the Uley Bury hill. Romantic as the manor is, it is an unlikely place for her to rest, even assuming she had the time. It is a long way from her army's route and very close to where Edward was soon to pass. The

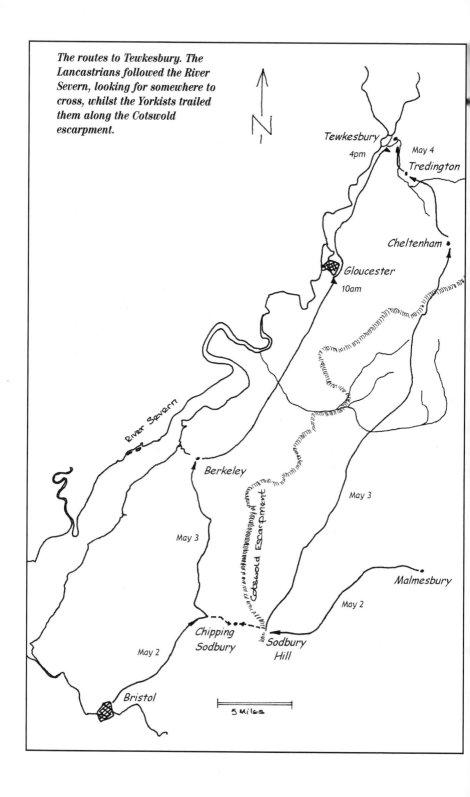

The routes to Tewkesbury. The Lancastrians followed the River Severn, looking for somewhere to cross, whilst the Yorkists trailed them along the Cotswold escarpment.

N

Tewkesbury
4pm
May 4
Tredington

Cheltenham

Gloucester
10am

River Severn

Berkeley

May 3

May 3

Cotswold Escarpment

Malmesbury

May 2

Chipping Sodbury
May 2

Sodbury Hill

Bristol

5 Miles

foundation for this story seems to be a letter in the possession of the owners of Owlpen, from Edward Prince of Wales, written upon his arrival in England to John Daunt, keeper of the royal park at Mere in Wiltshire. This summoned him to Edward's aid against 'Edward Earl of March, the King's great rebel'. The letter was at Owlpen because John's son John married Margery, heiress to the estate. Quite a tenuous basis for believing the queen slept there!

King Edward followed through the Cotswolds, in a quite different sort of country. While the Lancastrians travelled in wooded country in the vale, the Yorkists were on the open wolds – Champion Country. (This is an English corruption of 'Champagne', describing the open nature of the French region.) The Cotswolds was sheep country and sheep were the main generator of England's income in the fifteenth century. The road Edward would have followed from Sodbury Hill is now the A46. Even today it is recognisable as a drove road, with its very wide verges. This was far better ground for travelling, and Edward made very rapid progress. Nicholas Harpsfield, the author of the *Arrivall*, was probably in the rear of the army, and made some heartfelt complaints, which reflect the problems of foot soldiers and followers of armies on forced marches:

'which his people might not find, in all the way, horse food or man's food nor so much as drink for their horses, save for one little brook, which was full little relief, it was soon troubled with the carriages that had passed it.'

King Edward's messengers beat the Lancastrians to Gloucester, and Richard Beauchamp, governor, was ready for them. The instruction he had received was that he should keep the town for King Edward and defend it against the Lancastrians who were coming. Edward promised that he was on the way to 'rescue and comfort' the town if it were attacked. It is hard to describe the mood of the Lancastrians, having struggled night and day to reach this refuge, where they knew that the townspeople were well disposed to the cause and where they could rest and retrench before the next phase of their plan, to find that the gates were locked against them. The *Arrivall* says, with great understatement, that 'Of this demeaning they took right great displeasure.'

They made a token show of attacking the town, and given time they would probably have prevailed, because the garrison does not seem to have been very large and the town was generally hostile to the Yorkist cause. Both attackers and defenders knew that they would not succeed, because King Edward was close with his army and his spies were watching the situation as it developed. The Lancastrians quickly, and wearily, moved on to their only contingency plan – to continue north along the Severn and to find another crossing place.

Like most walled towns Gloucester was quite compact. The army had arrived at the Southgate and had to make their way around the outside of the walls to the Northgate road. This probably did not present many practical problems, if they kept far enough away, avoiding snipers on the walls. The weary army was in some disorder, though, the mounted men being well ahead of the foot soldiers, and those struggling along at the back with the supplies and the guns. Edward Hall's Chronicle says that as the last of the gunners dragged their burdens past the town, Richard Beauchamp took advantage of the lack of an armed escort to ambush them and capture some of the guns which they had detoured to Bristol to collect, and which had been dragged so far with so much effort.

The road to Tewkesbury must have seemed interminably long. To keep in touch with the river, and with the faint hope of finding somewhere to ford it along the way, the army probably took the Sandhurst road from Gloucester, and thence went through Wainlodes and Deerhurst. There was nowhere to cross. From Deerhurst, the road north took them to Tewkesbury, where they arrived at about four o'clock, following a road which was far from ideal for the army, and which was 'all in lanes and stony ways, betwixt woods, without any good refreshing'.

Tewkesbury presented them with a whole new set of problems. The hoped-for fording of the river at Lower Lode was not possible, so the onward route had to be through Tewkesbury and along the river. There was a bridge at Upton-on-Severn, but before they could reach this they would need to cross the Avon, which joins the Severn north of Tewkesbury. This was not an easy venture. The bridge was a complicated mix of two stone bridges, over two branches of the river, and a long wooden causeway crossing the flood plain to the foot of the Mythe Hill half a mile away. The bridge was narrow and never in

King John's Bridge. The difficulties of crossing this bridge led to the Lancastrians making their stand at Tewkesbury.

good repair, as there were constant quarrels about who was responsible for its maintenance. To get to the bridge, they had to pass through the narrow streets of Tewkesbury, where there would have been temptation and opportunity for men to simply slip away. There was also the danger that the Yorkists would come upon them when they were half-way across, which would mean certain defeat, and they knew that Edward was very close.

'And, for as much as the greater part of their host were footmen, the other part of the host, when they were coming to Tewkesbury, could, nor might, have laboured any further, but if they would wilfully have forsaken and left their footmen behind them, and thereto themselves that were horsemen were right weary of that journey, as so were their horses. So, whether it were of their election and goodwill or no, but that they were verily compelled to bide by two causes; one was for weariness of their people, which they supposed not their people would have any longer endured; another for they knew well that the King ever approached towards them, nearer and nearer, ever ready, in good array and ordnance, to have pursued and fallen upon them, if they would any further have gone, and, peradventure, to their most disadvantage.'

King Edward's army knew their destination and picked the best route towards it. He established a surveillance system, with spies and messengers, so that Margaret would not give him the slip again. His route would have been planned to be as flat and easy as possible and so probably swung well to the east to avoid the Stroud valleys, approaching Cheltenham through Bisley, Birdlip and Leckhampton Hill. At Cheltenham, he got news of the Lancastrian arrival in Tewkesbury. Significantly, the *Arrivall* says that the king paused for a little refreshing in his march, and shared with the army such food and drink as he had carried in the supplies wagons before starting on the way to Tewkesbury. This suggests that he no longer had to hurry; the Lancastrians were where he intended, and his only task remaining for the day was to make camp whilst the daylight remained. The refreshed army made its way through Bishop's Cleeve and Stoke Orchard towards the field of battle. Camp was made at Tredington, within three miles of Tewkesbury.

Both sides now knew the time and the place of battle. The outcome must have been the subject of a great deal of prayer.

Chapter Four

TEWKESBURY

THE LANCASTRIAN army's arrival in Tewkesbury must have caused huge consternation. Being conveniently half-way between Gloucester and Worcester, both important administrative centres, and possessing its own Abbey, Tewkesbury was used to lodging the occasional dignitary and even royalty, but the arrival of a whole army headed by a queen and the heir to the throne was in a different league altogether. The expected arrival of another army, headed by a rival king, must have taxed the diplomatic skills of the abbot.

Without the benefit of hindsight which we now possess there was a huge doubt about the outcome of the battle, many commentators at the time advising that the Lancastrians were the

Tewkesbury Abbey. The Abbey church dominates the town. The view shows the Swilgate in the foreground and is taken over the land once occupied by the refectory and cloisters.

stronger force. A report from Bruges to the Duke of Milan, in an irony of history, dated 7 May, says:

> 'A Spaniard, who left London on 24th April, relates that King Edward has set out with his power to look for the queen and the prince, who had landed and gone to the parts of Wales. We have heard nothing since, although we are greedy for news. There are many who consider the queen's prospects favourable, chiefly because of the death of the Earl of Warwick, because it is reckoned she ought to have many lords in her favour, who intended to resist her because they were enemies of Warwick.'

And this was from the court which financed King Edward's return.

Tewkesbury had been in the lordship of powerful national figures since before the Conquest. With the death of the last Despenser of the male line fifty years earlier the honour had passed through the female line to Warwick the Kingmaker. After his death at Barnet it passed to George, Duke of Clarence by virtue of his marriage to Warwick's eldest daughter, Isabel. As Clarence was now reconciled with his brother, Tewkesbury was officially Yorkist. Tenuous as this link may be, the town did seem to go against the general Lancastrian tendency of the region by holding Yorkist sympathies. This would have been a factor in the Lancastrian choice of battleground and in the abbot's attitude to these visitors.

Tewkesbury grew because of its location at the confluence of the Severn and the Avon, the major rivers of the Welsh Marches and the West Midlands. Though there was no bridge over the Severn there were seasonal fords and ferries. The Avon bridge is on the ancient road between Gloucester and Worcester. The town's viability came from trade, manufacturing and agriculture. Although large by the standards of the time it probably had a population of no more than 1,000 people.

Physically and economically it was dominated by its abbey. A Benedictine house, Tewkesbury was one of the richest foundations in England and had all the attributes appropriate to its status. There would have been between thirty and forty resident monks headed by Abbot Strensham and a much larger number of lay brothers and servants. The abbey owned much property in the town and the surrounding area, including a considerable amount of farm land. The church itself dominated the town, providing a

The abbey cottages. Built as a speculative venture by the abbey, these merchant cottages were occupied at the time of the battle.

landmark for travellers for many miles. The monastery buildings occupied a great deal of space and were surrounded by walls, except where protected by the River Swilgate.

The street layout in the town remains, with the three main streets following the same lines augmented by the winding ancient Saxon roads following the river. The agricultural nature of society was emphasised by the presence of a large open field, the Oldbury, behind the houses fronting Barton Street and High Street and common pasture lands between Barton Street and the Swilgate.

The town had no walls but was effectively protected by its rivers and streams. All roads into the town passed over bridges and because of the low-lying ground were frequently made

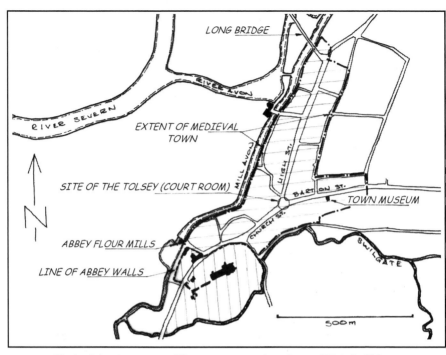

Tewkesbury town centre. The street pattern has changed little in 500 years, though the buildings have.

impassable by flooding or waterlogging. The southern boundary, which the Lancastrians would have approached, was protected by the Swilgate. The bridging point was at Holm Bridge, overlooked by the ruins of an old manor house on Windmill Hill. It was probably a drawbridge providing some protection against unwanted visitors at night and possibly against unwanted royal armies.

When the Lancastrians arrived they considered their options. Continuing their march was out of the question, so it was a matter of deciding on the best place to spend the night. Passing through the town and over the Avon presented too many difficulties, tempting though it must have been to attempt to gain the high ground of the Mythe Hill and Shuthonger Common. South of the Swilgate there were a number of possibilities; the deer park, where the Lord's manor house was

sited, Windmill Hill, site of the old manor house, or the fields in the vicinity. The *Arrivall* says:

'And, for that intent, the same night, they pight them in a field, in a close even, at the town's end; the town, and the Abbey, at their backs; afore them, and upon every hand of them, foul lanes, and deep dykes, and many hedges, with hills, and valleys, a right evil place to approach, as could well have been devised.'

Detailed as it is about the landscape, it could be describing any of the possible sites and we have to turn to John Leland for more clues.

At the time of the dissolution of the monasteries John Leland had a commission from Henry VIII to:

'diligently search all the libraries of monasteries and colleges of this realm, to the intent that the monuments of ancient writers might be brought out of deadly darkness to lively light'.

He visited Tewkesbury in 1540 and noted a book written by a monk in about 1476, which included a family history of the Earls of Warwick who were closely associated with Tewkesbury and the abbey. He noted the battle of Barnet, where Warwick the

The Gastons. The hedge to the right is that defended by Edmund Beaufort, Duke of Somerset.

Somerset's Lines

Kingmaker and his brother were killed, and then in the same year, *'Edwardus Princeps Henrici 6 filius venit cum exercitu ad Theokesbyri, et intravit campum nominee Gastum'* (Prince Edward son of Henry VI came to Tewkesbury with an army and entered the field called Gaston).

This could imply that Edward's army (though modern writers accept Queen Margaret as the Lancastrian driving force, contemporary writers were much more comfortable with her son as leader) set up their camp in the field called Gaston, or it could refer to the alternative meaning of field as battlefield. A further reference is to the 'Battle of Gaston near Tewkesbury'.

Gaston was a field of about forty acres, meeting the description in the *Arrivall*, and located alongside Lincoln Green Lane, one of the routes to Gloucester, though probably not the one followed by the bulk of the army. It would be an easy field to 'enter into', and there is a certain amount of logic in making camp on the site you

The Bell Hotel. This site on the edge of the abbey precinct has long given hospitality to travellers.

propose to defend on the next day. On balance the Gaston seems the most likely campsite. Since it was enclosed and divided in the seventeenth century, the fields so formed have been referred to collectively as 'the Gastons'.

Stories about Queen Margaret's lodging for the night abound. Chief candidates are Gupshill Manor and the Bell Hotel. Gupshill Manor certainly existed at the time, and was in the ownership of the Danvers family, possibly relatives of Agnes née Danvers, wife of John, Lord Wenlock. She could have played on family sympathies and procured beds for the night. The Bell Hotel is on the site of the old abbey lodging house, where

Somerset's front line. The hedge has been dated and found to predate the battle.

strangers and lay visitors would be accommodated. Despite misgivings, it is hard to imagine that the abbott would refuse a direct request for lodgings. Given the situation and with knowledge of Queen Margaret's character, it is hard to imagine that she would lodge herself so far from her men. Possibly her ladies would have spent the night in beds but she is likely to have been wide awake in a pavilion erected on the Gaston, poring over battle plans and tactics with the Duke of Somerset and other field commanders. There was not a lot of time and the future of the crown, no less, depended on the preparations they were able to make for battle the next day.

Despite their exhaustion, the army knew that it could not relax. Even if they had the opportunity, it is unlikely that anyone would be able to rest. First they would have looked to their stomachs. They had been without a meal for two exhausting days and a night. Alongside the Gaston was the Lord of the Manor's deer park. There would have been a lot of poaching of deer and rabbit that night. Arms and armour needed to be clean, sharp and in good repair. Directions from sergeants and the distribution of arrows from the supply wagons brought home the gravity of the situation, if they needed reminding. Bowstrings were checked, armour straps tested, joints greased, and blades honed. All this was done within earshot of the Yorkist army on this quiet spring night, grimly going through the same rituals. Next, they needed to look to their souls. There were no illusions about what might happen and it was important to be confessed and shriven, ready for the eventuality that the next day might be their last. Should any time be left before dawn they might rest.

Margaret's commanders surveyed the land and decided tactics. There was much to do in preparing defences and trying to predict what the enemy might do, in order to have counter-measures. Though they had been driven to Tewkesbury and cornered they had the advantage of choosing the field and preparing the ground for the battle. They chose the Gaston as their fortress. The southerly hedge was in part also the route of the Southwick brook, small but deep and muddy enough to form a barrier, and to defend the right flank of the army. Half a mile to the east was the Swilgate, a brook sufficient to defend the left flank. Between these two was a continuous line of field hedges, which were strengthened where necessary with stakes and such materials as they found in the vicinity. This was to be the Lancastrian fortress. The soldiers set about the task of preparing it for the coming onslaught.

Yorkist spies would have watched these preparations and reported back to Edward who was probably in council with his own commanders trying to predict his enemy's tactics and deciding his own. All in all, the Yorkists would have had a more relaxed time than the Lancastrians. Though they had not chosen the place, they were in full control of the time.

A campaign encampment. This camp at a re-enactment of the battle is probably much grander than the real thing.

Chapter Five

THE BATTLE OF TEWKESBURY
Saturday 4 May 1471

T HE LANCASTRIAN ARMY must have been up and in position at the crack of dawn. They would have known what happened at Barnet a few weeks earlier, where fighting had started as soon as silhouettes could be seen through the morning gloom. Despite the anxious eyes of her scouts trained on the enemy camp to give warning, Queen Margaret could take no chances. Her army had to be ready and alert.

This was not going to be an Agincourt with the armies exposed to

Initial battle dispositions. The Yorkists entered the field from the south and made their dispositions out of the direct view of the Lancastrian army.

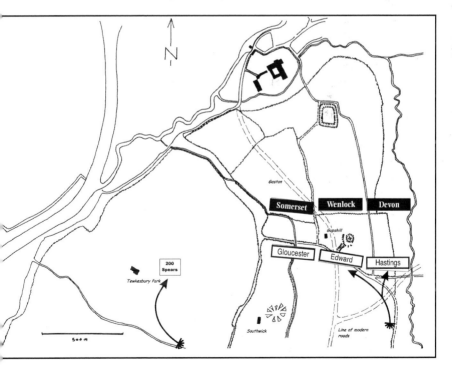

each other over open land. The Lancastrians would not have been so confident in their strength and they had not planned a showdown at this early stage in their campaign. Margaret's army used every bit of available natural defence and Edward was going to have to find a means of exposing them before he could attack. The *Arrivall* describes the site:

'In the front of their field were so evil lanes, and deep dykes, so many hedges, trees, and bushes, that it was right hard to approach them near, and come to hands.'

The army used the formation which had stood the English in good stead for centuries and would continue for centuries to come. They formed three 'battles' or wards: the van, centre and rear, to confront their Yorkist equivalents when they arrived on the field. The Lancastrian vanward was placed on the right, positioned within the Gaston field, with the Southwick brook to their right and Lincoln Green and the deer park beyond. This battle was commanded by Edmund Beaufort, Duke of Somerset, who was also Margaret's commander in the field. The rearward, against the Swilgate, was commanded by Sir John Courtenay, Earl of Devonshire.

The mainward, in the centre of the army, was more of a problem for Margaret. The command had to be given to her son Edward, Prince of Wales, but at eighteen years of age he had never been involved in a major battle. For much of his life he had lived in France, away from the factional politics of the English nobility. His youth was balanced by the experience of two mentors; John, Lord Wenlock of Somries, a veteran of the Hundred Years War, and Sir John Langstrother, prior of the Order of St John of Jerusalem.

We have the names of some seventy men who were with the Lancastrian army, most of whom would have been armed and ready in the early dawn. Many, like Sir John Arundel, Sir Seintclere Pomeroy and Sir John Daunt had their estates in the West Country. Others came from far away. Sir William Lermouth was a Northumbrian knight. Among the most notable was Edmund Beaufort's brother, Sir John, Marquis of Dorset. There were non-combatants who had arrived with the queen from France: Dr John Morton, Bishop of Ely, and Dr Ralph Makerell, vicar of Risby.

They waited through the dawn and early morning, peering through the hedges into the gloom, searching the horizon towards Stonehill, which they knew was where they would catch first sight of the enemy. They were waiting to fight for their lives, and the Lancastrian succession.

At Tredington, meanwhile, there was no urgency. Edward knew that the Lancastrians were not going to slip away and he had time to prepare properly. Mass was important. Food, too, was important and the army would have breakfasted on whatever the land could provide. There was a psychological advantage in delay and every advantage was valuable.

In their own time, the Yorkist army marched to the field of battle following the road from Tredington. The road crossed the Swilgate by the mill at Tredington, and then ran along the meadows by the river before diverging from the river to cross the ridge of Longdon Hill at Stonehill and passing south of Gupshill Manor to join Lincoln Green Lane. This road ran parallel to the Lancastrian front line, about 200 yards from it. The hedges and banks of this road would provide good forward positions for the Yorkists.

From Stonehill, the Gaston is overshadowed by the bulk of Tewkesbury Park, the deer park, and Edward expected this to play some part in Lancastrian planning. It was clear that it was not the chosen battlefield, but it could be used for an ambush. The Lancastrian army had used such a tactic ten years earlier at the battle of Towton. He despatched a force of 200 mounted knights to check:

> 'upon the right hand of their field there was a park, and therein much wood, and he, thinking to purvey a remedy in case his said enemies had laid any ambush in that wood, of horsemen he chose, out of his fellowship, two hundred spears, and set them in a plomp, together, near a quarter of a mile from the

The conflict opened with six 'battles' facing each other across the hedge of the Gaston, and 200 Yorkists 'spears' hidden in the woodland of Tewkesbury Park.

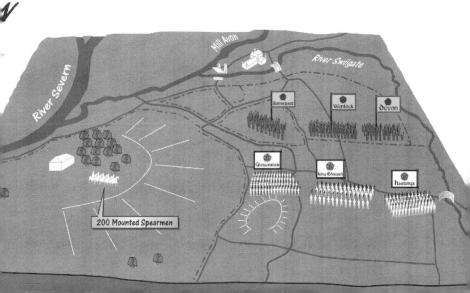

field, giving them charge to have good eye upon that corner of the wood, in case that any need were, and to put them in service, and if they saw non such, as they thought most behovefull for time and space, to employ themselves in the best wise they could.'

They must have used a wide detour to avoid the eyes of the Lancastrians. There were, surprisingly, no Lancastrians hidden in the park.

Six thousand men cannot arrive on the field simultaneously. The Yorkist battles had been arrayed at Tredington:

'The King apparelled himself, and all his host set in good array; ordained three wards; displayed his banners; did blow up the trumpets; committed his caws and quarrel to Almighty God, to our most blessed lady his mother, Virgin Mary, the glorious martyr Sent George, and all the saints; and advanced, directly upon his enemies.'

They must have reached the field over a period of an hour or more. The vanward was led to the field by Edward's youngest brother, Richard, Duke of Gloucester. His place was facing the Duke of Somerset. His arrival in the field took him, just out of bowshot, across the front of the Lancastrian centre and vanward. This was an opportunity for an intimidating display with much beating of drums, blowing of trumpets, displaying of banners and posturing. Gloucester's arrival must have taken some time, as getting men and their equipment into position is no simple task. Their position was along the hedges and banks lining the road. Once in position they waited for their orders. The other wards followed, King Edward facing the Prince of Wales and his mentors in the centre and John, Lord Hastings, opposing the Earl of Devonshire.

We have the names of over 100 Yorkists who fought in the battle. Predominantly, but by no means exclusively, they were from the Home Counties and Midlands. Fighting alongside Edward, though, were Sir John and Sir Phillip Courtenay from Devon, cousins of the Earl of Devonshire. Queen Elizabeth Woodville's son, Sir Thomas Grey, was present, with several other Grey family members, who ten years earlier had been committed Lancastrians. Sir John Mowbray, Duke of Norfolk, Earl Marshal of England and a lifelong Yorkist and father and son Sir Edward and Sir George Neville, cousins of the Kingmaker, were also marching with King Edward's army.

There was no parley here to see if a peace could be agreed and avoid the battle. Edward did not intend the Lancastrian leadership to leave the field alive and Margaret had similar sentiments about the Yorkists.

The Duke of Gloucester led the Yorkists into battle and the assault. The Lancastrians held a strong position, not easy to approach, but they were in no position to fight a defensive battle. Only the Yorkists could win that way. Edward played upon Somerset's known impetuosity. The Yorkist army was by far the better equipped with ordnance. They had brought mercenary gunners with them from Flanders, where the art of gunnery was more advanced than in England. They had also robbed the Lancastrians of much of their own fire power with the attack at Gloucester and these guns may now have been turned against the men who had dragged them step by step from Bristol.

'Nevertheless the King's ordnance was so conveniently laid afore them, and his vanward sore oppressed them, with shot of arrows, that they gave them right-a-sharp shower. Also they did again-ward to them, both with shot of arrows and guns, whereof nevertheless they had not so great plenty as had the King.'

The battle opened with a bang. Guns would not have been familiar to most of the army, and the sound, smell and sight must have been intimidating. It must have reminded them of what they had been told about Hell from the pulpit. This was a premonition of what was to come. The guns and arrows were aimed at Somerset. Though the range was necessarily long, and guns were neither accurate nor consistent, the Yorkist supremacy in numbers began to tell and the action became more one of attrition. No matter how inaccurate, if enough random missiles are fired into the lines men will be killed or wounded. They will also be made fearful, feeling that they have no control of their destiny. The Lancastrians had no response to this assault. Somerset knew that cowering behind his defences and seeing his men maimed one by one was not the route to victory. He had to take the initiative:

'But Edmond, called Duke of Somerset, having that day the vanward, whether it were for that he and his fellowship were sore annoyed in the place where they were, as well with gun-shot, as with shot of arrows, which they neither would nor durst abide, or else, of great heart and courage, knightly and manly advanced himself, with his fellowship, somewhat aside-hand the King's vanward, and, by certain paths and ways therefore afore purveyed, and to the King's party unknown, he departed out of the field, passed a lane, and came into a fayre place, or close, even afore the king where he was embattled, and, from the hill that was in one of the closes, he set right fiercely upon the end of the King's battle. The King, full manly, set forth even upon them, entered and wane the dyke, upon them, into the close, and, with great violence, put them up towards the hill, and, so also, the King's vanward, being in the rule of the Duke of Gloucester.'

It is unlikely that this manoeuvre was spontaneous, as the Lancastrians would not have expected to win the battle with purely defensive tactics. There had to be an offensive move, and there had to be a plan, discussed at length with Queen Margaret through the night. This was probably the first part of it and it would have been familiar to all the other commanders.

The 'certain paths' must have been Lincoln Green Lane, then a road to Deerhurst and ultimately to Gloucester. Some of the army could have trodden this track on the way to Tewkesbury on the previous day. Running along the bottom of the shallow valley between the park and the ridge now occupied by the Yorkist army, it was hidden from the Yorkists by the trees and bushes growing in the badly drained and uncultivated valley bottom. The 'hill that was in one of the closes' is there today a few hundred yards down the lane. Being on the edge of their front line, the Lancastrians would have surveyed this track on the evening before and prepared plans to utilise it.

The Lancastrians mount an attack on the Yorkist flank, which is repelled, then attacked and scattered by the 200 spearmen.

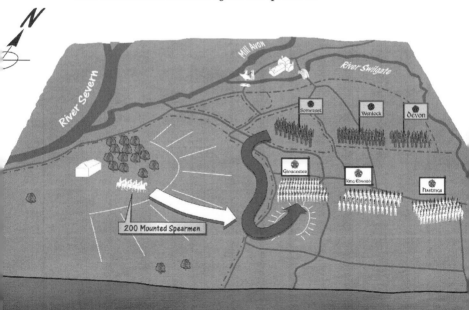

The need for stealth suggests that not all of Somerset's division was deployed. The 'fellowship' was probably a small group of hand-picked men. The manoeuvre would make more sense if they were mounted and this would resolve a lot of the problems there are in understanding the action. There is nothing in the accounts of the battle, or any of the many subsequent analyses, to say if they were on horseback or not, unless the use of the word 'fellowship' is intended to mean a mounted group. However, when discussing the Yorkist group sent to the deer park, the *Arrivall* states specifically that they were horsemen.

Somerset's mission in isolation was unlikely to win the battle but it would create a diversion to allow time and space for the other divisions to act. It was a considerable gamble, to take the commander away from his command to attack 'the end of the king's battle', knowing that he would lose contact once he had passed behind the Yorkists. It was a tortuous path, passing close to, if not between, elements of the Yorkist army. A strict interpretation of the text suggests that Somerset attacked the centre of the Yorkist army, which he reached either by passing between the centre and van wards or by outflanking the army and attacking from the rear. This latter is the most plausible, but suggests a weakness of Gloucester's flank defences. Attacking Edward directly with a small élite group would have been an obvious tactic if the opportunity presented itself, because the battle would be won if Edward fell. Gloucester himself

The Yorkists advance into the Gaston, pushing the Lancastrians back until they eventually break and flee.

was later to attempt the same at Bosworth against Henry Tudor.

Not only was it a desperate move but it was also a trap. Edward's 200 spears were watching the battle unfold below them, awaiting an opportunity to intervene. They must have seen Somerset's move but chose not to react. The thick and well-maintained hedge surrounding the park was the probable reason. This would be too difficult a barrier to negotiate at a gallop and, without the element of surprise, they had no advantage. They chose to wait.

Somerset's heroic gambit inevitably failed. Having gained the brow of the hill, his fellowship had no choice but to expose itself and charge down the slope. On foot, this would have been both slow and noisy and there could not have been a lot of surprise left by the time they struck the king's ward. They were driven back by Edward into the hands of Richard. Fighting desperately hand-to-hand the fellowship retreated, not towards their own lines, from which they were cut off, but back towards the park, where they hoped to find some respite in the difficult ground among the trees. They may also have hoped to draw some of the Yorkist force away from the battle, as had happened at Barnet, where Oxford left the field to pursue Lord Hastings. This was not to be, however.

> 'Which provision came as well to point at this time of the battle as could well have been devised, for the said spears of the King's party, seeing no likeliness of any ambush in the said wood-corner, seeing also good opportunity to employ them self well, came and brake on, all at once, upon the Duke of Somerset and his vanward, aside-hand, unadvised, whereof they, seeing the King gave them enough to do before them, were greatly dismayed and abashed, and so took them to flight into the park.'

Once through the park hedges, in an environment designed for charging downhill along wide grassy rides, the horsemen found the fellowship easy prey. The surprise was complete. Somerset had been comprehensively outmanoeuvred by Edward and his attack ended in total confusion and rout. They fled in all directions, with Yorkists in pursuit. Many were wounded, taken or slain.

The Duke of Somerset seems to have escaped back to his command. Though contemporary accounts make no mention of it, Edward Hall's *Union of the Noble and Illustrious Families of Lancaster and York*, published in 1542 under a Tudor king, contains a note that Somerset sought out Lord Wenlock and, calling him traitor, struck the brains out of his head with his battleaxe. Though this is unlikely to have happened, it does reflect the lack of support the rest of the Lancastrians gave to Somerset's diversion, and the suspicion that Wenlock was somehow responsible and even in the pay of the Yorkists. Wenlock is listed among those slain in the battle.

Having beaten off Somerset's fellowship with little difficulty, King Edward immediately went on to the offensive. He ordered a general advance of the army and in short time had taken the defensive hedges and ditches. The Lancastrians were now fighting a desperate, hand-to-hand battle on the Gaston field and losing ground. The whole line was engaged and soon broke in confusion, with men fleeing the field in every possible direction:

> 'the king courageously set upon that other field, where was chief Edward, called Prince, and, in short while, put him to discomfiture and flight, and so fell in the chase of them that many of them were slain, and, namely, at a millstream, in the meadow fast by the town, many were drowned, many ran towards the town; many to the church; to the Abbey; and elsewhere, as best they might.'

The mêlée quickly degenerated into a rout. Discipline in the Lancastrian lines collapsed and individual soldiers fled from the field in desperate panic and confusion with no aim beyond immediate self-preservation. In their triumph and with humanity cast aside, the Yorkists engaged in a ruthless and merciless pursuit, hacking down their prey as swiftly as they could be cornered:

> 'In the winning of the field such as abode hand strokes were slain incontinent [impatiently, without thought]; Edward, called Prince, was taken, fleeing to the town wards, and slain, in the field.'

At this point, the whole purpose of the Lancastrian cause was gone. The last of the Lancastrian line was dead, and the war was lost.

The death of Prince Edward. Copied from the Ghent manuscript. It is purely conjectural.

The ground the Lancastrians had chosen to defend proved hostile to an

55

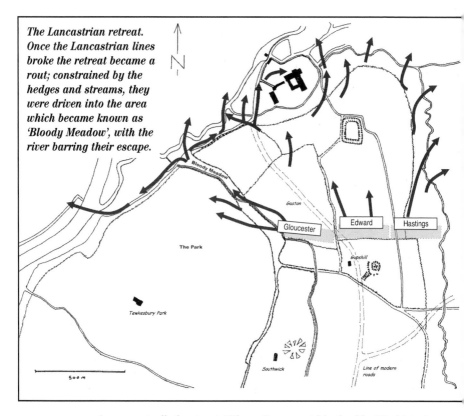

The Lancastrian retreat. Once the Lancastrian lines broke the retreat became a rout; constrained by the hedges and streams, they were driven into the area which became known as 'Bloody Meadow', with the river barring their escape.

army in uncontrolled retreat. Where it was not blocked by Yorkists it was surrounded by water. The rivers and streams were not only deep but also muddy with slippery banks and wet margins. This slowed the fleeing Lancastrians, and many were caught. Many were simply trampled into the soft mud by the press of panicking escaping soldiers.

A retreat turned rout presents a far more dangerous and costly threat to an army than a pitched battle or even fighting withdrawal. It is no surprise that casualties amongst both leaders and ranks of the Lancastrian army were far higher than among their Yorkist opponents. Prince Edward must have been caught up in this, and other notable Lancastrians, recorded as slain, were probably swept up in the panic. Among them were two of the leadership: John Beaufort, Marquis of Dorset and brother of Edmund, Duke of Somerset, and Sir John Courtenay, Earl of Devonshire, who commanded the Lancastrian left. Among others slain were Sir Edward Hampden of Beckley, Sir John Lewkenor of West Grinstead,

Sir William Vaux of Harrowden and Sir John Delves of Doddington, whose son was caught and beheaded. There is no record of any Yorkist notables dying in battle.

Lancastrian troops fleeing from the vanward of their broken army would have been desperately trying to reach the safety of the town or the wide green spaces of Tewkesbury Ham, visible beyond Lower Lode Lane and the Mill Avon. As they ran back from the Gaston field, the Southwick brook on one side and the impenetrable hedge bordering the Lord's land on the other funnelled them into a marshy meadow, part of the old road system linking Lincoln Green and Lower Lode Lane. Unable to escape to either side and with the soft ground slowing the flight they were at the mercy of their pursuers. The ensuing carnage gives the field the name by which it has been known ever since – the Bloody Meadow.

Crossing the fields between Tewkesbury town and the Gaston field and passing in front of the abbey is the Swilgate, which flows into the Mill Avon just beyond Lower Lode Lane. For those who managed to escape the field of battle towards the town, there were only two bridges across the Swilgate: Holm Bridge on the main road and Gander Lane Bridge, at the far end of the abbey precinct. Beyond that the Swilgate could be forded, but for many of the exhausted and beaten Lancastrians, weighed down with armour and with their assailants at their backs, it proved an insurmountable hurdle and they were either cut down on its banks or drowned as they attempted to cross.

The abbey church, too, was a tempting refuge. John Warkworth's Chronicle has Lancastrians being pursued into the church and King Edward himself appearing there, with sword drawn. The priest celebrating mass was drawn into the mêlée in an attempt to stop the possible slaughter. Sanctuary was claimed by the fugitives, who included the Duke of Somerset and Sir John Langstrother, prior of the Order of St John. There then came a difficult stand-off between the abbey and the crown. Edward wanted prisoners, but the sanctuary of the church had to be respected, entrenched as it was in traditions as old as the common law itself. The rights and freedoms of the Church were jealously guarded by Rome. Abbot Strensham faced a dilemma. Edward was undisputedly now the king. The abbey survived by noble patronage and the abbot was politician enough to know that his interests would not be advanced by crossing the king. A compromise was agreed. The abbot accepted that the abbey did not have the freedom to grant sanctuary to the king's traitors; the king agreed to their pardon. The *Arrivall* treats the abbey's resistance with contempt:

> 'And where there were fled into the said church many of his rebels, in great number, hoping there to have been relieved and saved from bodily harm, he gave them all his free pardon, albeit that there never was, never had not at any time been granted, any franchise to that place for any offenders against their prince having recourse thither, but that it had been lawful to the King to have commanded them to have been drawn out of the church, and have done them to be executed as his traitors, if so had been his pleasure.'

The nobles were immediately arrested, but there must have been lots of ordinary soldiers who were released and sent back to their villages.

Frightened and exhausted men sought refuge in nooks and crannies all over Tewkesbury and were sought out by their pursuers. This gave an excuse for looting and Tewkesbury, which had done nothing to aid the Lancastrians, was sacked by the victorious Yorkists. Undoubtedly atrocities were committed but they involved the common people and so were not recorded.

Lancastrians fled and were pursued for long distances. There is a record of the desecration caused at the parish church of Didbrook, some ten miles from Tewkesbury, on no direct route, where the Bishop of Worcester held an inquiry twelve months later because the church had been 'notoriously polluted by violence and the shedding of blood'. Here, the drastic step of demolishing the church and completely rebuilding it seems to have been taken, at the expense of the abbot of the nearby Hailes Abbey.

Queen Margaret took no part in the battle itself but watched it anxiously, with her entourage of ladies and clerics, from the rear. Local tradition says that she watched from the tower of the abbey. Although there is a view over most of the site from there, it is an unlikely choice. Much more likely is the high ground of Holm, or Windmill, Hill. This is

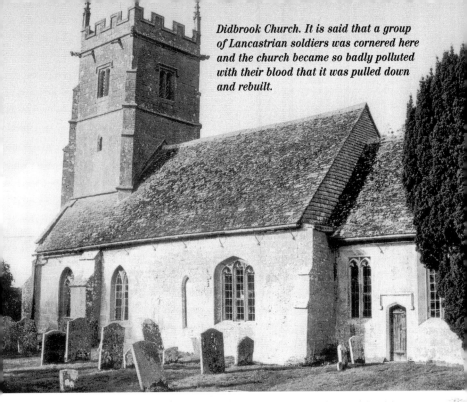

Didbrook Church. It is said that a group of Lancastrian soldiers was cornered here and the church became so badly polluted with their blood that it was pulled down and rebuilt.

Lower Lode. The ancient crossing point on the Severn, forded by the fleeing Margaret – all her hopes and dreams shattered following the death of her son in battle.

immediately behind the Gaston, with a panoramic view of the battlefield, and she could be in easy communication with her army. She would have been most anxious about the safety of her son, upon whom all hopes for a Lancastrian future rested. The hill also had a windmill, from which, in like manner to Edward III at the battle of Crécy, she could survey the field from a height. As defeat became a certainty, and possibly on the news of the death of her son, she slipped away down Lower Lode Lane to the River Severn, where she was shown by two monks how to ford it on horseback. She disappeared into the wilds of Malvern Chase.

King Edward had cause to celebrate. He had won his second battle against a Lancastrian force within three weeks and the Lancastrian power base had been destroyed forever. He went to the abbey for a thanksgiving mass. Writing in the early twentieth century, a local author, Mr Bradley-Birt, presents a melodramatic picture:

'The king, in generous mood, gave his word and then formally received by the abbot, joined the great procession of knights, soldiers and monks through the "church and the quire to the high altar where with great devotion he was praising God and yielding up unto him convenient laud".

'It must surely have been the strangest scene that the old abbey in all its long history has ever witnessed. One moment filled with the clash of arms, the shouts of the victors and the cries of the wounded and the dying, the next hushed to silence at the bidding of the victorious king. The long procession led by the abbot with the consecrated Host still in his hand, jostles up the full length of the abbey over the bodies of the vanquished that strewed the nave right up to the high altar, the magnificent figure of Edward of York, triumphant, dominating the scene. Once more the silence is broken. This time it is the sound of prayer and praise, of thanksgiving for victory, a hastily improvised service for which there could have been no previous preparation. With what feelings did the abbot conduct the service, and with what heartiness did the monks render the responses, thanksgiving for the final defeat of the Lancastrian dynasty, which had proved itself so good a friend to the Church, thanksgiving for the Yorkist king whose devotion was suspect, whose leanings were towards the hated Lollards? And with what feelings, huddled out of sight in a corner of the abbey, must Somerset, the Prior of St John and others whose hopes lay in the dust and who still clung to their refuge within the abbey

Tewkesbury Abbey Church. A view from what was the north-eastern end of the Gaston.

as their one chance of life, have listened to this service of praise and thanksgiving? Surely the most tragic service that has ever been held within the abbey walls.'

Having thanked God for his victory, he thanked his army by knighting some forty men on the field. The ceremony is said to have taken place in the 'Knight's Field, near the village of Grafton'. Grafton must be a mis-transcription of Gaston. It is easy to mistake 'f' and 's' in old manuscripts. Why it is described as a village is not known. The name 'Knight's Field' has not come to us in field names, either in documents or oral tradition.

After the events of Saturday 4 May 1471 came the reflection of Sunday 5 May. The Yorkists gave thanks. The dead, mostly Lancastrian, were prepared for burial or, in the case of the common men, were buried where they had fallen, 'naked' (stripped of armour and anything valuable) and without much ceremony, in large pits. The Lancastrian prisoners considered their likely fates. The Lancastrian fugitives made good their escape.

Chapter Six

THE ELIMINATION OF THE LANCASTRIANS

O N THE DAY FOLLOWING the battle, Edward must have looked back on the events with immense satisfaction. Everything had gone to plan. In fact, there could have been little to cause him concern in the outcome. Edward, Prince of Wales and the Lancastrian heir, was dead and with him the Lancastrian succession. There was no one of royal blood in John of Gaunt's line with a legal claim to the throne. Edmund Beaufort, Duke of Somerset (also descended from John of Gaunt though debarred from the succession by Act of Parliament), was in his custody. He was the last legitimate Beaufort in the male line, the last of the family which had held such power over King Henry, and been so hostile to Yorkist aspirations. Queen Margaret was gone, fleeing towards Wales and the friendly lands of Jasper Tudor, Earl of Pembroke, who she hoped would assist her to return to France.

Jasper Tudor himself had failed to reinforce the Lancastrians, thanks to the work of Richard Beauchamp in keeping Gloucester secure. He had reached as far as Chepstow with his forces but because of the barrier of the River Severn was unable to join the Lancastrian force at Tewkesbury. Now that the cause was leaderless, all he could do was return to West Wales and plan for his future. Neither England nor Wales offered any security and he soon took the road to Brittany, with his young nephew Henry Tudor.

There were immediate problems to be solved in Tewkesbury, in the form of a number of prisoners, including some dyed-in-the-wool Lancastrians, and in particular Edmund Beaufort. The chronicles take different lines on the promises Edward had given to Abbot Strensham to secure their custody from the sanctuary of the abbey, but it is reasonable to suppose that the later accounts are as biased against Edward's integrity as the early ones are in support of it. The author of the *Arrivall* has no doubts about the legitimacy of what he did:

'This battle thus done and achieved, and the king's grace thus largely shown, it was so that, in the Abbey, and other places in the town, were found Edmund, called Duke of Somerset, the Prior of St John's, called Sir John Langstrother, Sir Thomas

Tresham, Sir Gervaise of Clifton, knights, squires and diverse other notable persons, which all, diverse times, were brought before the King's brother, the Duke of Gloucester and Constable of England, and the Duke of Norfolk, Marshal of England, their judges; and so were judged to death, in the midst of the town, Edmund Duke of Somerset, and the said prior of St John's, with many other gentils that there were taken, and that of long time had provoked and continued the great rebellion that so long had endured in the land against the King, and contrary to the wellbeing of the realm. The said Duke, and others thus judged, were executed in the midst of the town, upon a scaffold therefore made, beheaded every one, and without any dismembering, or setting up, licensed to be buried.'

This summary justice does not measure well against our current concepts, but this was a political trial and there was no attempt to disguise it. The prisoners would doubtless argue that their treason was only in the eye of the Yorkist party and that they were loyal to a legitimate king who was still alive, though incarcerated by the usurpers. Pragmatically, though, they would have known what their fate was to be. These were all men who had been offered the hand of friendship during the ten years of Yorkist rule, but had plotted and rebelled. The author of the *Arrivall* has no sympathy at all. If the boot had been on the other foot the Lancastrians would have been equally harsh.

The usual punishment for treason was hanging, drawing and quartering. In summary, this involved being dragged around the town on a hurdle and hoisted up by the neck, rather than dropped into a pit in a way designed to bring a quick death. The art was in keeping the traitor alive, cutting him down, reviving him and then opening up his body to draw out the entrails, finally causing death. The corpse was then beheaded and cut into four quarters, which were sent to the four corners of the kingdom to be set up for public display in the major cities.

Edward's father had been killed at Wakefield, and had been posthumously beheaded, his head bedecked with a paper crown and set up on Micklegate Bar in York. Edward must have recalled this and there must have been a temptation for further revenge, which he characteristically resisted. The traitors were simply to be beheaded. There was to be no mutilation and no setting up. The bodies would be released for burial in consecrated ground. This was mercy beyond

Edward IV surrounded by his court. Kneeling before him are Sir William Herbert and his wife. Sir William was the Yorkist Earl of Pembroke. Surprisingly, Henry Tudor grew up in his household until he became a political pawn after Tewkesbury.

In this picture of the endgame of the battle, Graham Turner shows King Edward's banner leading the way through the hedge onto the defending Lancastrians in the blue and white livery of Edmund Beaufort, whose portcullis badge flies on a banner. In the distance are the Yorkist standards

of Gloucester, Clarence and Norfolk. The diversity of arms and armour is evident, as is the difficulty of discerning friend from foe. The advantage of polearms, where there is space to wield them, and the advantage of fighting in teams, can be clearly seen.

An illustration from the Ghent manuscript depicting the climax of the battle. Behind the archers, King Edward is seen unmounting a Lancastrian knight and Edward, Prince of Wales is being cut down and killed, probably by Clarence or Gloucester.

The Ghent manuscript depicts the execution of the Lancastrian leadership. Sir Edmund Beaufort, Duke of Somerset is seen on the block. Heading the queue awaiting their turn is Sir John Langstrother, Prior of the Order of St John of Jerusalem and treasurer to the Lancastrian king.

View of the deerpark, now a golf course, from the Abbey tower. The Swilgate is in the foreground, and the brick buildings occupy the site which Lieutenant Colonel Blythe thought was Holm Castle.

BLOODY MEADOW   DEER PARK   HOLM CASTLE

SWILGATE

reasonable expectation and probably part of a planned approach to settling the unrest in the land. Tewkesbury is notable even amongst the conflicts of the Wars of the Roses for the number of executions following the battle, clearly intended to remove all possible catalysts for future rebellion. Tempering this with mercy signalled that this was the end of the family feuds which had caused so much division among the peerage throughout King Henry's life.

The judges, then, were Yorkists who had both fought in the battle, one of them the king's brother. The court-house was in Tewkesbury's civic building, the Tolsey, or toll house for the market, which stood where the cross now stands. The scaffold was erected nearby, in Church Street. There would have been no doubt about the verdict. These men had all been fighting against the king, so the case was open and shut and the verdict inevitable. There was no appeal. The outcome, though, was in the king's prerogative. Only the king could overturn the sentence and offer a pardon. Many were pardoned without trial, particularly those who had supported the cause because of an affinity with a Lord. These men were not seen as a threat to the crown and pardons brought revenue with them, as they involved a hefty fine. The *Ghent Manuscript*, an account of the battle written for Edward's continental supporters, contains a list of the dead at the battle, and at the end of a list of fourteen who were beheaded appears the single entry '*Guillame Crymisby jugut a mort et pardonne*' ('William Grimsby condemned to death and pardoned'). Who William Grimsby was, and why he was pardoned, we don't know. The Warkworth Chronicle, which is not quite contemporary, and was written at a distance from the events described, says that Grimsby was executed.

The number of dead in the battle and its aftermath is a matter of conjecture, just as the size of the armies is. All that is certain is that they were nearly all Lancastrian. Numbers would be at best in the high hundreds, at worst in the low thousands. With an army of 6,000 it is very unlikely that the dead would have exceeded 1,500. Men would have died later, often months later, of wounds received in the battle, which would often be very deep and infected. Sir Seintclere Pomeroy of Berry Pomeroy died on 31 May, Sir William Boteler of Warrington on 8 June. Probably the abbey infirmary was overflowing with the badly injured.

Those who fell on the battlefield would have been looted by the victors and others for anything of value on their person, including not only money but boots and such weapons and pieces of armour that they possessed. The stripped bodies, naked or in ragged underclothes, were left on the field. Shallow grave pits were dug in places which needed minimum effort, using existing pits and ditches if possible, and heaping the earth up to form mounds over the bodies. This was probably a task undertaken by Lancastrian prisoners. If not they, then the local people would have had to attend to the task, if only to limit the stench of death and the despoliation of bodies by birds and wild animals. Such men were afforded scant dignity in death.

The higher classes fared better. King Edward had allowed burial to be at the choice of the dead or their families. The abbey was the choice for many, though some were buried elsewhere. The body of Sir John Langstrother, prior of St John's was 'enclosed in lead and taken to his own place'. Henry Barrow and the Delves, father and son, were buried in the abbey church but afterwards 'taken from there to their own country', once their family received news of their whereabouts. Most of the named people killed or executed still lie in the abbey. Interestingly, the burial place of John, Lord Wenlock, is uncertain. It is recorded that he was taken from the field to be buried but there is no record of his grave in the abbey, and his family chapel at St Mary's, Luton, contains a memorial but not a tomb.

Queen Margaret's flight from Tewkesbury and over the Severn at Lower Lode took her through the densely wooded countryside of the Malvern Chase. Her destination would have been safe Lancastrian territory, probably deep in Wales, whence she could make her escape to France in due course. She was hardly travelling in secret. She was accompanied by a party which included her ladies: her daughter-in-law Anne, Lady Katherine Vaux and Margaret, Countess of Devonshire. All of these had lost husbands or sons in the battle, though probably they did not know this. It is likely that the party also included Dr Ralph Makerell and Dr John Morton, both companions of Queen Margaret, and William Joseph, the king's secretary, who were all pardoned after the battle (in Joseph's case seven months afterwards) but unlikely to have been involved in the fighting. There is a local tradition that the party spent the first night following the battle at Payne's Place, the home of a sympathiser, close to the Lower Lode crossing. This seems unlikely as Margaret would have been anxious to put distance between herself and the Yorkists, and unless her escape was in the early evening – also unlikely – spending an anxious afternoon close to the battlefield would have been folly. We next hear of her from the *Arrivall*:

66

Tewkesbury Cross and Church Street. Once the site of the market house, scene of the trial of the Lancastrians. The scaffold was erected in Church Street.

Payne's Place. Built in about 1450 by Thomas Payne, a supporter of Warwick the Kingmaker. There is a legend that Margaret spent the night here after the battle.

'All these things being done, the Tuesday, the seventh day of May, the King departed from Tewkesbury, towards his city of Worcester, and, on the way, he had certain knowledge that Queen Margaret was found not far from there, in a poor religious place, where she had hid herself, for the surety of her person, the Saturday, early in the morning, after her son Edward, called Prince, was gone to the field, for to withdraw herself from the adventure of the battle; of whom also he was assured that she should be at his commandment.'

There is an inconsistency in this account. Given her past record and character, it is unlikely that Margaret would have left the battlefield early in the morning before the battle when she could have safely stayed behind the lines, close to her son. This apparent error can be explained by the Yorkist nature of the account, and the lack of detailed information about the Lancastrians available to the author. The universally accepted view is that the 'poor religious place' was Little Malvern Priory, some fourteen miles from Tewkesbury. After the battle she would have taken steps towards safety, not cowered in the first refuge she found. Fourteen miles in two days for a very conspicuous group of people, fugitives, travelling through the dark and dangerous lanes of an extensive hunting ground, seems reasonable progress.

It was Sir William Stanley who had caught Margaret's party at Little Malvern and he took her to King Edward, who by now had moved from Worcester to Coventry, concerned about news of a rising in the North. She was by now a broken woman, the death of her son marking the end of all her ambition. She was paraded by Edward on his return to London, and incarcerated in the Tower until it was expedient to ransom her to King Louis XI as a pawn in another of the French king's plots.

Edward's haste to leave Tewkesbury was due to reports of rebellion in the North. He went quickly to Worcester and then on to Coventry, where he began the process of raising yet another army to face this new threat. This came to nothing, though. In a welcome show of loyalty the Earl of Northumberland arrived in person with the news that the North submitted to Edward. This was a decision forced by the lack of a charismatic leader and knowledge of the outcome at Tewkesbury. Northumberland was rewarded with a commission to return to the North and maintain the peace.

Not all of England was at peace, however. Thomas Neville, the Bastard of Fauconberg, a nephew of Warwick the Kingmaker, had been given charge of Warwick's fleet of ships. He had spent the period of the unrest cruising the Channel, doubtless following his uncle's profession of piracy. He had taken no active part in the struggle for the crown although he might have been charged with intercepting Edward leaving Flanders. If he was, he not only failed but was so ineffectual that his attempt was unworthy of record.

For reasons which are not clear, Thomas Neville landed in Kent with troops from the Calais garrison at about the time when Edward was waiting for the Lancastrians at Sodbury Hill. He raised an army in Kent, where men seemed always ready to rebel. They marched to

Little Malvern Priory. Sheltered under the Malvern Hills, this is generally accepted as being the 'poor House of Religion' where Margaret surrendered to Sir William Stanley.

London, where the city resisted their entry, resulting in a siege which went on for some days, despite the news from Tewkesbury. After failing in their attempts to storm the gates, the rebels were driven back and retreated into Kent, and thence to Calais.

Just as London was being cleared of the final challenges to his regime, King Edward arrived. He entered the city with great ceremony. Accompanied by his army with banners displayed he marched from Shoreditch to St Paul's. The procession was headed by Richard, Duke of Gloucester. At the rear was a carriage carrying the captive Queen Margaret, bound for the Tower.

Later on the same day, 21 May, King Henry VI died. There was little attempt to disguise what happened to him. The *Arrivall* says that he died of pure displeasure and melancholy on hearing the news from Tewkesbury, but John Warkworth presents a different picture:

'And the same night that King Edward came into London, King Henry, being inward in person in the Tower of London, was put to death, the twenty first day of May, on a Tuesday night, between eleven and twelve of the clock, being then at the Tower the Duke of Gloucester, brother to King Edward, and many others; and on the morrow he was chested and brought to Paul's, and his face was open that every man might see him; and in his lying he bled on the pavement there; and afterwards at the Blackfriars was brought, and he bled new and fresh; and from thence he was carried to Chertsey Abbey in a boat, and buried there in Our Lady Chapel.'

The Milanese Ambassador to the French Court reported to his master that:

'King Edward has not chosen to have custody of King Henry any longer, although he was in some sense innocent, and there was no great fear about his proceedings, the prince his son and

A nineteenth-century photograph of the Tower of London. Henry VI was secretly assassinated here following the Yorkist victory at Tewkesbury.

the Earl of Warwick being dead as well as all those who were for him and had any vigour, as he has caused King Henry to be secretly assassinated in the Tower, where he was a prisoner. They say he has done the same to the queen, King Henry's wife. He has, in short, chosen to crush the seed.'

The information about the queen was wrong.

Richard, Duke of Gloucester, was probably at the Tower in his role of Constable of England to carry out King Edward's orders but his involvement in the deed is unlikely to extend to wielding the blade. The truth has been lost in propaganda and counter-propaganda. Many commentators report on rumours of Richard's involvement in the murder, including Polydore Virgil and the Great Chronicle of London. It was also reported that miracles took place at Henry's tomb in Chertsey.

This was the end of the Lancastrian dynasty. Edward was secure on the throne of England, which he held until his death, and now able to concentrate on the traditional obsession of medieval English kings: gaining possession of France.

EXPLORING THE BATTLEFIELD

Advice to Tourers

Tewkesbury lies in the borderland between the Midlands and the West Country, midway between Birmingham and Bristol. It is very conveniently located, about a mile from Junction 9 on the M5 motorway, served by Ashchurch railway station, and with a frequent bus service to Cheltenham. The general area is covered by OS Landranger™ map number 150.

The town has a compact and historic centre, with the battlefield within very easy walking distance. There are several hotels and lots of bed and breakfast establishments in the town. The Bell Hotel, in Church Street, is built within the old monastery precinct, probably occupying a site which has offered hospitality to travellers for hundreds of years. The Abbey Hotel and the Royal Hop Pole are also in Church Street; the latter is an old coaching inn. Tewkesbury Park Hotel lies a little out of the centre but stands in the middle of the old deer park, now a golf course. The 200 Yorkist mounted spearmen were concealed near the present-day hotel, which is built on the foundations of the old manor house, though nothing of the medieval building remains today. Close to the abbey and the town centre is a Caravan Club site.

All the hotels have bars and restaurants. There are numerous daytime tea-rooms and cafés in the town. The abbey Refectory and the Abbey Tea Rooms, opposite it in Church Street, offer good quality and value. For evening meals, the Berkeley Arms provides good home cooking and well-kept beer. My Great Grandfather's and the Rendezvous restaurants, again in Church Street, provide a good range of English cuisine. There are Indian and Chinese restaurants in the town but for something a little different the reputation of the New World Vietnamese restaurant in High Street attracts customers from far and wide.

The best general guidebook for the area is the *AA Leisure Guide of the Cotswolds*. There are a number of books of local landscape and historical interest available at bookshops in the town. The OS Explorer™ map 190 shows Tewkesbury and the battlefield, in detail. Unfortunately, Tewkesbury is not central to the map and Tredington, associated with the Yorkist overnight camp, is shown on map number 179.

The battlefield and sites associated with it are spread over a wide area south of the town. Much of this is accessible and the

Battlefield Walk

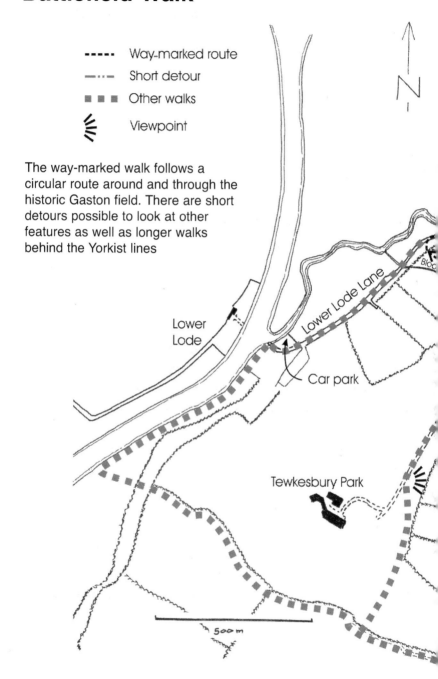

-----	Way-marked route
—··—	Short detour
■ ■ ■	Other walks
≣	Viewpoint

The way-marked walk follows a circular route around and through the historic Gaston field. There are short detours possible to look at other features as well as longer walks behind the Yorkist lines

Lower Lode Lane

Lower Lode

Car park

Tewkesbury Park

N

500 m

START

Abbey

Holm
Bridge

Obelisk

The Gastons

Queen
Margaret's
Camp

Gupshill
Manor

Lincoln Green Lane

The
Hillock

To Tredington

Tourist Information Centre in Barton Street has a 'battle trail' leaflet which contains a useful plan of the battlefield, with footpaths and a way-marked battlefield walk. The leaflet describes an anti-clockwise walk. Experience has shown that going round in a clockwise direction is preferable and visits key points in the battle landscape in a proper sequence. This walk is described below.

Walking the Battlefield

The most convenient starting point for the walk is Gander Lane, leaving Church Street past the abbey car park and crossing the bridge over the Swilgate onto the Vineyards, now the town recreation ground. Alongside the footpath up the slope are the bowls club and the rugby club. These have been built in an area which was full of wide ditches and called 'the Moats'. It was levelled after the Second World War by using it as a convenient landfill site. Though there are claims for its being the site of a grand house and a defensible position potentially used by the Lancastrians, it is likely that this was the site of the abbey's fishponds. Large quantities of carp and bream were reared to satisfy the needs of meatless days.

At the top of the field, on the right of the path, is a low obelisk. This was erected in 1932, when the area was opened to the public. There are four inscriptions, one of which perpetuates the story that this was the site of Holm Castle. Dr Anthea Jones' research shows that there was a house there in the sixteenth century, but there is very little other information about it. Looking back towards the town from this point there are splendid views of the abbey. The buildings before you are a mere shadow of what once stood there. The clues to the demolished monastery can be seen in the walls. Between the monastery and the Swilgate stood the meaner buildings, workshops and lay buildings. Monasteries displayed outward signs of great opulence. This was the era of the visions of Piers Plowman. The Church tried to give a glimpse of St John the Divine's vision of the New Jerusalem to downtrodden peasants in the majesty of its foundations. Tewkesbury was no exception. It was big. It was walled. It was colour-washed. It had a spire above the tower, reaching another hundred feet towards heaven. It was a sight designed to remind men of who they were and what they were. It was the first sight of Tewkesbury from the south, visible for many miles, and must have created a strong impression on the men who fought in the battle.

Looking beyond the sports pitches to the left is Holm Bridge

Erected on the site of vineyards of the abbey, the obelisk commemorates, among other things, the battle of Tewkesbury.

THIS INSCRIPTION COMMEMORATES THE
FACT THAT TEWKESBURY ABBEY
DATING FROM THE 11TH CENTURY
CONDEMNED BY THE COMMISSIONERS
OF HENRY VIII TO BE DESTROYED
WAS PURCHASED BY THE BURGESSES
OF TEWKESBURY IN 1543 FOR £483
THE MANOR OF TEWKESBURY WAS
PURCHASED BY THE CORPORATION
FROM JAMES I IN 1609 OR £2453

where the main road crosses the Swilgate, much altered and raised well above the natural level, but in the same position as in 1471, when it was likely to have been a drawbridge. South of it is the slope of Holm Hill, or Windmill Hill. On the far side of the road is the eminence once occupied by Leland's 'Holm Castle'. On the near side, the slope is identified with the field briefly called Battylham. Would this be a suitable site for Edward to show his gratitude and publicly knight his supporters?

In some interpretations of the battle, the higher ground from Holm Hill across the Vineyards was the Lancastrian front line, which would put the Obelisk, as one of the panels says, in the midst of the battlefield. This is a largely discredited view, though.

The way-marked trail now passes along a footpath between the cemetery and a housing estate. This is the old lane skirting the edge of the old Gaston, the route towards Tredington and thence to Cheltenham. The Gaston had been divided into seven fields by the seventeenth century. The cemetery was created in two of them by the Victorians. Further down the lane the cemetery gives way to housing and to Abbots Road, built to provide access for Edwardian housing development. The way-marked trail uses Abbots Road and Gloucester Road, the seventeenth-century turnpike which bisected the Gaston, to reach the two remaining Gaston fields.

An alternative, longer, route is to cross Abbots Road, where the footpath continues behind the houses, reaching Gloucester Road close to the southern point of the old Gaston. On the opposite side of the road you can see where the path used to continue towards Gupshill, where it met the Cheltenham road. Strolling south along the road brings you to Queen Margaret's Camp, an earthwork believed to be the remains of an early medieval moated house, probably demolished long before the battle. This high land provides a good view over the southern part of the

Detail from the battle model in Tewkesbury museum.

battlefield. The road which Edward followed ran immediately south, up from the Swilgate valley and crossing south of the Gupshill buildings to join Lincoln Green Lane. West can be seen the deer

The Gastons today: the Lancastrian view to the Yorkist lines.

YORKISTS

LANCASTRIANS

Hillock

The view from Queen Margaret's camp towards the hillock and the Yorkist lines.

park, where he sent the 200 spears who ambushed Somerset. North were the hedges defended by the Lancastrians, almost all of which have disappeared beneath gardens now. The Gaston hedges defended by the Duke of Somerset's division are hidden behind the Gupshill manor, off to the north-west.

As an extension of the way-marked walk, a short stroll south along the main road brings you to the footpath to Queen Margaret's Camp. (As this is immediately opposite the Gupshill Manor Inn, it is a good refreshment point, and it is also easy to visit by car.) The 'camp' itself is a moated site, with no trace of any buildings remaining. The track to what is believed to have been a yeoman's house remains as a hollow way. It joined the road which ran from what is now a housing estate to Lincoln Green Lane past the opposite side of Gupshill Manor to the present road. The views of the early battle positions are good from Queen Margaret's Camp.

Yorkist route and lines

Looking towards Gupshill Manor is to look between the front lines. The Lancastrians were to the right, behind the hedges of the Gaston, which are still discernable despite development. The Yorkists were on the left, their line extending from the foot of the deer park hill through the housing estate down to the Swilgate river beyond. In the near distance is the hillock used by Somerset.

There are no public footpaths from here into the battlefield, so returning to the way-marked trail involves a walk along Gloucester Road to the gate of the Gastons on the left of the road.

The view from the higher land by the field gate is towards where the Yorkists formed their lines in

Gupshill Manor buildings today. The remnant of a larger complex which was partially destroyed by fire. It is now a public house.

Old road and Yorkist line

King Edward's position. The old road ran in the foreground, the Yorkists arrayed behind it. View of Yorkist position from the Gupshill.

the broad shallow valley. Beyond, the hillock down which Somerset charged can be clearly seen. The 'secret way', Lincoln Green Lane, is not obvious at all, though its route can be guessed by the groups of houses which have been built alongside it. There are only two fields left undeveloped today and it is not possible to get a proper impression of the wide open spaces of the fifteenth-century field, now hedged in and built upon. What is missing is the sense of scale. Five or six thousand men trekked exhausted into this field and immediately started to prepare to fight for their lives.

The footpath takes you down the slope towards the Southwick brook, which runs alongside the hedge. This was Somerset's part of the line, which Richard, Duke of Gloucester bombarded with 'shot of gun' and 'right a sharp shower' of arrows. The stile at the foot of the field leads out into Lincoln Green, now much reduced by building and enclosure. Opposite are the lower slopes of the deer park.

Back in the Gastons, the way-marked track leaves the field along a path between a farmyard and the modern housing, crossing a

footbridge over the brook into a long, narrow field bordering Lincoln Green Lane. This field was part of the old road, before it was metalled and confined. Passing through this field, the route crosses Lincoln Green Lane on the stretch which used to mark the northern limit of the Gaston, the hedge through which the Lancastrians spilled in their desperate retreat, fighting hand-to-hand through the Gaston until they had nowhere left to retreat. Beyond this lane was the solid hedge of the Lord of the Manor's land on Holm Hill. The only easy route was into what is now called the Bloody Meadow, another long, narrow field, but this one strongly hedged on either side.

The way-marked route passes into the Bloody Meadow. At the entrance is a plinth containing an interpretation panel explaining a little of the battle and the protagonists. It suffers a little from using poorly contrasting colours and trying to show two possible sets of troop positions. This makes it confusing. The Bloody Meadow itself is an atmospheric place, particularly at dusk. It has always been

The interpretation panel was erected in the Bloody Meadow in 1985 to mark the opening of the way-marked walk.

Legend has it that the Bloody Meadow was the scene of the fiercest slaughter as the retreating Lancastrians were cornered.

marginal agricultural land, has not been farmed for many years and apart from being better drained it is probably not very different from the fifteenth-century field. It is easy to see how the fleeing Lancastrians would have been slowed and trapped in this area, pushed together by the shape of the field and with no easy escape.

The path passes through the Bloody Meadow and on to Lower Lode Lane. Here there are views of the wide open spaces of the Severn flood plain. The River Swilgate, here in a deeper and wider bed, is a considerable barrier. The walk turns right towards Tewkesbury. This is the old road from Gloucester. Just before it meets the Gloucester Road there is a pumping station – not an attractive feature, but it is here that excavations in the middle of the

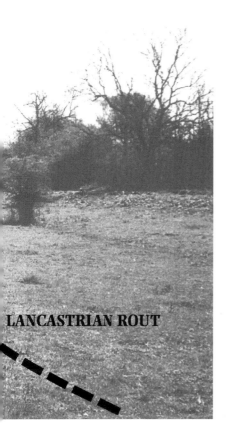

LANCASTRIAN ROUT

nineteenth century to improve the town's sewerage system revealed human bones, which are likely to have been from bodies of drowned men pulled from the river and buried in a mass grave. This could not have been the only grave pit but there is no evidence of others having been found.

The route turns towards the town on Gloucester Road. It is worth examining the bridge over the Swilgate in passing. On the right, the original ground level can be seen. Here there is a great deal of landscape alteration to reduce the effects of flooding on transport. The bridge has been altered and widened several times over the years. There are remnants of earlier bridges to be seen in the structure but probably not the medieval bridge, which is likely to have been a drawbridge.

From here the old road deviated to the left of the modern road to skirt the abbey precinct. It passed through what is now the car park and into the Victoria Gardens. This area was also heavily built up and reclaimed to create a garden to commemorate Queen Victoria's jubilee. When the current road was made, by widening the gap at the Bell Hotel to accommodate stage coaches, the area fell into disuse. Immediately upon entering the gardens there is a path to the right which leads to the abbey gatehouse. This was the main entrance to the precinct. The old abbey wall is still visible on the right of the gardens and at its end is the barn where grain was stored for the watermill. The present Abbey Mill building is of a far later date.

At the end of Victoria Gardens a right turn leads into Mill Street

Margaret's escape

Lower Lode Lane, the road to Tewkesbury from Gloucester and the Severn crossing.

Lincoln Green Lane was 'the secret way' used by Somerset to outflank the Yorkists.

Somerset's 'Secret Way'

and to Church Street. The timber-framed buildings on the right were first built at around about the time of the battle, along the line of the abbey wall.

And so the walk arrives back at the starting point, with plenty of choice of refreshment nearby.

As well as the detour described to Queen Margaret's Camp, there are other associated sites which are easily accessible. Lincoln Green Lane is best explored on foot. It gets progressively narrower until it becomes a footpath. Look out for the footpath to the left, which passes Ten Acre Cottages and skirts the Duke of Somerset's hillock. There is no short circular route back so the best option is to retrace your steps to Lincoln Green Lane. Continuing down the lane, through the trees and out into the field beyond, there is a footpath crossroads at the end of the field. A right turn leads into Tewkesbury Park, the old deer park. The path skirts the golf course and eventually rejoins Lincoln Green Lane at the park gates. The views here over the battlefield are those seen by the Yorkist horsemen, looking down on Somerset's manoeuvre.

Lower Lode Lane was the summer route to Tewkesbury. The lane now ends at the riverside, with a parking and picnic area and a ferry to the Lower Lode Inn on the opposite bank. It is from here that Margaret of Anjou was helped to ford the river by two monks and made her escape when all was lost. The footpath through the College Boat House grounds leads to the old riverbank road. This is now way-marked as the Severn Way to Deerhurst and beyond. After half a mile it is joined by a path coming down through the wood which marks the edge of the flood plain, along a very sunken roadway. Following this leads to the crossroads of paths south of the park, so Lincoln Green Lane can be used as the return leg of the walk.

Windmill Hill, or Holm Hill, features large in the battle, and particularly in alternative interpretations based on the existence of Holm Castle. The site is now occupied by Tewkesbury Borough Council's offices, so permission should be sought to visit it. The area has completely changed in character since 1975 and there is no impression at all of the unkempt field which was once there. The view remains, though. From the grassed area beyond the staff car park the entire battlefield can be seen, from the ridge at Queen Margaret's Camp and the height of the deer park to the Gaston field and the Bloody Meadow. It is now despoiled by housing but the impression remains. Here stood a windmill. This position must have

Lancastrian march

The riverside path that was once the road from Gloucester.

presented an extremely good viewpoint and of all the possibilities available seems the most likely for the Lancastrian rear position, the base for Queen Margaret and her entourage to anxiously view progress, with an escape route behind them if the worst happened.

In 1975 archaeological excavations revealed the presence of extensive high-status building on the hill, associated with Lords of the Manor up to the fourteenth century. Where the car park now stands was Leland's Holm Castle. This is the front line that was defended in Blythe's version of events, stretching across the road into the Vineyards, with the Yorkists attacking up the slope from the Gaston.

Appendix I

The Town, Abbey, Tredington and Sodbury Hill

When the Lancastrian fugitives fled to the abbey they would have sought sanctuary in the church, which still stands. There is no other evidence of sanctuary being sought in Tewkesbury Abbey in all its long history, and no artefacts equivalent to the Durham knocker or the chair at Beverley. We cannot know where they were lodged after being surrendered to Edward. Their court-house, the Tolsey, is long demolished, and there is no clue as to the location of the scaffold except that it was erected in the midst of the town. The likely choice is in Church Street.

There was a tradition in Tewkesbury that the Prince of Wales was captured by Sir Richard Crofts, who surrendered him to Edward. He was then murdered by Gloucester and Clarence in a house in Church Street, where there was said to be a bloodstain on the floor which could not be removed. This did not prevent its demolition, though. The site is now occupied by the Job Centre.

There are many connections with the battle in the abbey apart from the contrived juxtaposition of a Yorkist emblem and the Lancastrian heir in the choir. To view the plaque in the choir it is best to seek permission from a verger, as this is not an area where public wandering is encouraged. To view the armoured door of the sacristy, now the vestry, it will be necessary to seek permission in advance of a visit. Of the other associations, there is a second plaque to the Prince of Wales' memory fixed to the wall of the south transept and there is a plaque to the memory of the Courtenay dead, John, Hugh and Walter, fixed to the east wall of what is now the abbey shop, which once housed an altar to St James. Unfortunately this is now hidden by shelving.

The graves of the dead were probably never marked except for that of the Prince of Wales, who had a marble tombstone with inlaid brass. Most were recorded as being buried in the midst of the church, with many others, and no further detail. The church was divided into two by the rood screen. The western part was the parish church, the eastern the preserve of the clergy and monks. Those of lesser rank were buried in the parish church, with concentrations in front of the rood screen or in the churchyard. The disruption caused by the grave digging must have been immense.

89

Tewkesbury Museum, in Barton Street, contains a display associated with the battle, including an excellent model, made in 1971 at the 500th anniversary by a team of local people with expert support.

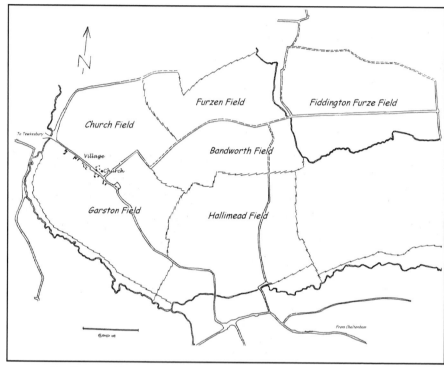

Tredington village showing the medieval field plan. Edward's camp is reputed to have been in the Garston field.

Tredington

The evidence for the Yorkist army spending a night at Tredington is very circumstantial. The only support comes from the *Arrivall*, which says 'Wherupon the Kynge made no longer taryenge. And set forthe towards his enemyes, and toke the fielde, and lodgyd hym selfe, and all his hooste, within three myle of them.' The case for Tredington is that it is within three miles of Tewkesbury, and that it lies on the old road from Cheltenham. Writing in 1830, James Bennett speculates that the encampment might have been at either Elmstone Hardwick or Tredington, so there is probably no oral tradition pre-dating this,

The old Garston field, Tredington, the probable site of the Yorkist camp.

and over time the Tredington faction has prevailed. It does seem the most likely location, with open field agriculture, within a short march of Tewkesbury and with a good view of the abbey.

Tredington was a small linear settlement scattered along the road, then as now. It operated a common field agricultural system using four fields: Church field, Garston field, Bandworth field and Furzen field. The villagers believe that the camp was in Garston, between the road and the Swilgate River. The similarity of the field name to 'Gaston' may have prompted this choice. The likelihood is that they would have chosen the field which was fallow that year. A claim that Edward spent the night in a barn in the field is reflected in 'York Barn', a recent barn conversion on the edge of the old field. Though none of the current buildings in the village are old enough to have lodged the king, he would undoubtedly have lodged in one of their predecessors – Tredington Court seeming a good candidate.

The little church of John the Baptist, then a chapel of ease, would certainly have been visited by the royal party and they must have taken mass there before leaving to join battle. There is nothing at all to commemorate the visit.

The march to Tewkesbury must have been on a broad front, using

Tredington church, then a chapel of ease and probably where Edward celebrated Mass before the battle.

both the track ways and the adjacent fields. There are still several footpaths, remnants of tracks into and through the fields, and the ancient 'Rudgeway' road, which bypasses Tewkesbury to the east. As the Swilgate stood between Edward and his enemies, he must have crossed it as soon as he could. The closest crossing was the bridge on the outskirts of Tredington. From there, there is now a footpath parallel to the modern road, linking with the old road past Queen Margaret's Camp and Gupshill Manor, which is the likely Yorkist front line. The path now runs through the 'Stonehills' housing estate but is easily found, and is a very pleasant hour's walk, though it tends to get sticky after rain.

The 'champion country' of the Cotswolds through which the Yorkists

Sodbury Hill

'The King, the same Thursday, soon after noon, came near to the same ground, called Sodbury Hill, and, not having any certainty of his enemies, sent his scowrers all about in the country, trusting by them to have news where they had been. About that place was a great and fair large plain, called a wold, and doubtful it was for to pass further, until he might hear something of them, supposing that they were right near, as so they might well have been, if they had kept forth the way they took out of Bristol. And, when he could not hear any certainty of them, he advanced forwards his whole battle, and lodged his vanward beyond the hill, in a valley toward the town of Sodbury, and lodged himself with the remnant of his host, at the same hill called Sodbury Hill. Early in the morning, soon after three of the clock, the King had certain tidings that they had taken their way by Berkeley toward Gloucester, as so they took indeed.'

So the *Arrivall* describes an episode which could have resulted in the battle of Sodbury Hill, but which was possibly the only Lancastrian feint to fool Edward.

As a place to do battle, the plain above the Cotswold escarpment at Sodbury would have suited very well. This was 'champion country, unenclosed and made over to sheep. Today it is arable land growing rape and wheat, but the impression of openness remains. The fact that Edward sent his van down the hill suggests that he might have been planning to confront them in the valley, which is still wide and open, even retaining wide areas of common land.

Sodbury Hill is not particularly easy to pin down, as the name is

The road along the valley from Chipping Sodbury, the place nominated for the battle by the Lancastrians.

not in current use and the whole ridge is of a consistent height. Sodbury probably refers to Chipping Sodbury, as the other candidates, Old and Little Sodbury would have been too small to be counted towns.

A good candidate for Edward's camp must be the large and secure iron age fort above Little Sodbury, as it offers some defence, a very good view of the valley and good ground around it for battle.

An alternative is the hill now marked by a large ventilation tower for the railway tunnel beneath. This has the advantage of having an associated valley 'towards the town of Sodbury', which follows the route now taken by the A432, where it drops down to Chipping Sodbury from its junction with the A46.

Visiting the area is best done on foot and involves some steep slopes. The roads around the hill are narrow and totally devoid of parking places. Good starting points are at Old Sodbury, where you can pick up the Cotswold Way, up the escarpment to the fort, and past the remains of a long-abandoned village. An alternative starting point is the Cross Hands Hotel, at the crossroads on the A46 and along the unclassified Hill Lane opposite. Views from here are limited, though.

Sodbury includes the Cotswolds, with Iron Age forts on the edge of the escarpment, a steep slope with two old settlements, including abandoned house sites and a wide open plain in the vale.

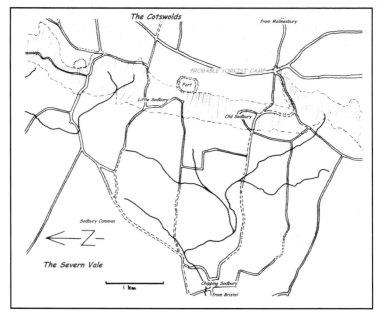

Appendix II

Biographical Sketches of Key Protagonists

King Edward IV

Edward Plantagenet was judged to be more handsome than any man alive. He must have been a very striking figure. When his statue was measured in 1789 it was found to be over six feet three inches long and broad in proportion. His household accounts show that he dressed richly and fashionably. He was said to be a man of prodigious appetites.

Edward was born at Rouen on 28 April 1442, eldest son of Richard of York and Cecily Neville, though recently there has been some doubt cast on his parentage. His upbringing is not well recorded but as heir to one of the greatest of the English aristocratic families he would have been taught the skills of hunting, fighting and chivalry

The Yorkist royal family being presented with one of Caxton's books by Earl Rivers, Edward's brother-in-law.

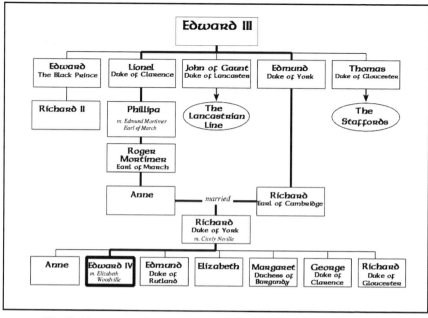

```
Edward III
```

| Edward The Black Prince | Lionel Duke of Clarence | John of Gaunt Duke of Lancaster | Edmund Duke of York | Thomas Duke of Gloucester |

| Richard II | Phillipa m. Edmund Mortimer Earl of March | The Lancastrian Line | | The Staffords |

Roger Mortimer Earl of March

Anne — married — Richard Earl of Cambridge

Richard Duke of York m. Cicely Neville

| Anne | Edward IV m. Elizabeth Woodville | Edmund Duke of Rutland | Elizabeth | Margaret Duchess of Burgundy | George Duke of Clarence | Richard Duke of Gloucester |

The Yorkist party claimed a superior line back to Edward III, through the

The sun in splendour badge, an emblem of the Yorkists.

which were essential to the ruling classes.

He must have been aware of the tensions between the king's party and his father from an early age and at the age of seventeen he was thrust into the developing struggle, escaping to Calais with his father and his allies after the debacle of Ludford Bridge in October 1459. After this events moved very quickly indeed. In June the following year he fought at Northampton. In December he was sent to raise troops at Ludlow, which is why he was not at Wakefield where his father and brother were killed on 30 December. He now assumed the leadership of the Yorkist cause and the title of Duke of York.

In February 1461, he led his army to victory at the battle of Mortimer's Cross. From there he met Warwick the Kingmaker and together they entered London and on 4 March Edward was declared king. He legitimised his position in the eyes of the world by his momentous victory at the battle of Towton on 29 March. He was crowned on 28 June.

At nineteen years of age Edward faced the tasks of subduing Lancastrian opposition to his rule and imposing his own style on the role of king, a role which had been diluted and corrupted by forty years of advisors to King Henry. Opposition was not properly subdued for several years.

Edward fell out with the Kingmaker. In part it was because of differing views of the policy to be followed towards France and general involvement as advisor, but it is generally acknowledged that Edward's impetuous and unwise choice of wife was the final straw. There can be little doubt that Edward married Elizabeth Woodville without a great deal of forethought and certainly with no advice. The justifications for his action are diverse. The outcome was to upset the very people he needed to cultivate and the situation did not improve as the Woodville family began their systematic climb up the ladder of wealth and power. Warwick the Kingmaker gave up on Edward in 1467 when a treaty he had negotiated with France was rejected in favour of an alliance with Burgundy and the marriage of Edward's sister Margaret to Charles, Duke of Burgundy. The Kingmaker turned to Edward's brother George, Duke of Clarence, a young and fickle protégé.

Edward was outwitted by the Kingmaker in 1469 and fell into his hands. The blood of several leading Yorkists was spilled but Warwick was unable to rule in the king's name without the consent of the king and Edward regained the upper hand. The rebels fled, eventually arriving at the French court and making their peace with the exiled Lancastrians.

Warwick's return forced Edward to flee to the Burgundian court, where he was less than welcome. It was only when Duke Charles learned of the Kingmaker's agreement with King Louis of France to declare war on Burgundy that he gave support to the Yorkist return to England.

Once the ripples of the Tewkesbury campaign had settled, England became more stable and prosperous. Edward himself maintained his appetites. France was invaded in 1475, the invasion was a military failure but it resulted in some financial gain, and the ransom of Queen Margaret. In 1478, George, Duke of Clarence, plotted one too many times, and was put to death for treason.

Edward became ill in 1483. His body was by then abused and gross, the result of years of lust and gluttony. He did not have the strength to recover and died on 9 April. It was in the aftermath of his death that the lack of wisdom in his choice of wife became most apparent, leading indirectly to the death of his sons and the fall of the Yorkist dynasty.

George, Duke of Clarence

George was the third son of Richard, Duke of York and Cecily Neville. Born in Dublin in 1449 whilst his father was effectively in exile as Lieutenant of Ireland, he must have absorbed the resentment of the Yorkists from a very early age. After an early

encounter with Queen Margaret at Ludlow in 1459, when he was captured with his mother and brother Richard after the Ludford Bridge incident, he was sent to Burgundy for safety, returning when Edward had secured the crown. Like Richard, he was given the trappings of a prince by Edward, including the title Duke of Clarence. In 1462, at the age of thirteen, he was appointed Lieutenant of Ireland, a post for which he was clearly unprepared. Because of his age and impressionability he fell completely under the influence of the Kingmaker, who had a hand in the guardianship of both of the king's younger brothers.

When Warwick the Kingmaker rebelled in 1469 it was with Clarence, who had been promised the crown. To cement this alliance, George married Isabel, Warwick's eldest daughter. This had been against Edward's wishes but George, who had seen his position as heir-apparent disappear with the birth of Edward's daughter Elizabeth, had had little luck in securing an heiress as a wife. He cannot have been happy to see all the eligible English heiresses contracted to marry the queen's relatives.

The rebellion ultimately failed and the conspirators fled to sea. Whist they were off Calais, negotiating with Lord Wenlock, Isabel went into labour, to the consternation of all. Clarence's first child was stillborn. Warwick's negotiations with Louis XI and Margaret of Anjou to support an invasion of England must have convinced Clarence that his opportunity to become king had passed and that he was now a support player in the drama. His sister Margaret, Duchess of Burgundy, was in secret contact with him and acted as the intermediary in a plan for him to return to his brother's favour.

Clarence returned to England with Warwick, who restored Henry to the throne and drove Edward into exile. Clarence bided his time. When Edward returned and marched south towards London with a small army and little support, Clarence intervened dramatically by delivering the four thousand troops he had arrayed for the Lancastrians to the Yorkist cause. The *Arrivall* describes the moment, in a field between Warwick and Banbury. The two armies met and arrayed. Between them the brothers met as if to parley. Clarence changed sides and trumpets were sounded in joy. He fought alongside Edward at Barnet and Tewkesbury.

Clarence was rewarded with his betrayed father-in-law's titles of Earl of Warwick and Salisbury but his avarice and ambition soon put him at loggerheads with his younger brother, Richard of Gloucester. He was so opposed to Richard's marriage to Warwick's younger daughter Anne, widow of the Lancastrian Prince Edward, that he abducted her. They fell to quarrelling about Warwick's inheritance.

King Edward lived with his brother's plots and insults over the years, but in 1478 Clarence went too far and was accused of conspiring to cause the king's death. He was tried and executed on 18 February 1478. Dominic Mancini and other contemporary commentators have it that he was drowned in a butt of sweet wine. The persistent tradition is that it was malmsey.

It has been said that Clarence was a 'family nuisance and a public liability'. He was handsome and eloquent but totally lacking in morals, scruples or judgement. Most agree that he deserves Shakespeare's description as 'False, fleeting, perjured Clarence'. Through his wife's inheritance, he became lord of the manor of Tewkesbury upon Warwick's death, a position confirmed by Edward in the division of the Warwick estates between him and Gloucester. Isabel's body was interred in Tewkesbury Abbey on her death in 1476. George, Duke of Clarence joined her two years later.

Joan Beaufort, daughter of John of Gaunt, linked the Nevilles to the royal family. Richard Neville's daughters reinforced the link by marrying the most eligible men in the land.

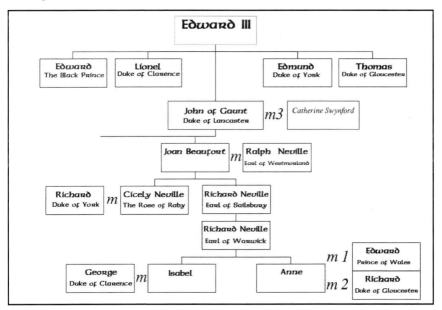

Richard, Duke of Gloucester

Richard was born in Fotheringay Castle on 2 November 1452 with, according to William Shakespeare, a full head of hair and a full set of teeth. Though intended as an insult, this in some way epitomises Richard. In sharp contrast to his Lancastrian cousin Edward, Prince of Wales, Richard did not talk and posture about military action; he learned quickly and developed competently from a remarkably young age.

Richard was the youngest of four brothers. In 1460, his world changed when his brother Edmund and his father were both killed at Wakefield. In the following year his oldest brother won the throne. He was quickly raised to the status of a prince, being created a Knight of the Bath and of the Garter, and Duke of Gloucester. He entered the household of Warwick the Kingmaker at Middleham Castle where he learned the duties which befitted his station.

When the Kingmaker rebelled in 1469, Richard did not follow his brother George, Duke of Clarence into the Lancastrian camp. He was loyal to Edward, going with him into exile in Flanders and back into England to retake the throne. He led the Yorkist right at the battle of Barnet, which he did so competently that he was entrusted with leading the vanguard of the army into battle at Tewkesbury and facing the Duke of Somerset, the Lancastrian commander. He was nineteen years old, the same age as his brother Edward was when he inherited the Yorkist mantle and led them to victory at Mortimer's Cross and Towton. Military leadership ran in the family.

After Tewkesbury, Richard became a vital part of the administration. He

Richard, Duke of Gloucester. Richard III, 1483 - 1485.

was given command of the North, a traditionally rebellious and quarrelsome area. He gained the support and respect of the northern magnates, particularly the Earl of Northumberland, and brought governance and order to the area.

In 1472, he married Anne Neville, the youngest daughter of the Kingmaker, and widow of Edward, Prince of Wales, killed at Tewkesbury. She was his cousin, and someone he had known since childhood. They had a son, Edward, who died in 1484. This marriage put him at odds over the Warwick inheritance with George, Duke of Clarence, who was married to Anne's sister Isabel. The brothers' treatment of the Dowager Countess of Warwick, their mother-in-law, was shoddy in the extreme.

He agitated for action against the Scots and in 1482 he was given leave to lead a large English army into Scotland. For many reasons this was not a success and a siege of Edinburgh Castle had to be abandoned. The one lasting outcome was the restoration to England of Berwick, ceded twenty-one years earlier by Queen Margaret. King Edward appeared satisfied by the outcome.

King Edward's sudden and unexpected death in April 1483, probably brought on by over-indulgence in the pleasures of the flesh, threw Richard into the limelight. Richard became Lord Protector during the minority of Edward V and all the pent-up antagonism arising from Queen Elizabeth Woodville's family connections and their desire for power spilled out into open hostility. Richard, Edward's most loyal supporter, made the surprising declaration that his brother's children were the illegitimate result of a bigamous marriage and in June 1483 he accepted the crown for himself as the legitimate heir, becoming King Richard III. Edward's sons never emerged from the Tower of London where they had been lodged. The possible fate of the Princes in the Tower has engaged every generation since.

Richard proved a good administrator, putting what he had learned in the North to good use, and set about reforming the law to the benefit of the common people. He could not escape the nature of his accession, however, and the alienation of powerful noblemen led to open rebellion in late 1483. The arrival of a Tudor army of invasion in 1485 culminated in the battle of Bosworth, Richard's death in the thick of the battle and the end of Plantagenet rule in England.

Richard's body was taken to Leicester without ceremony and buried in the Grey Friars chapel in Leicester. This was destroyed at the Reformation and no trace of his grave remains.

John, Lord Wenlock of Someries

John Wenlock had a very long and eventful life by fifteenth-century standards.

Born in or before 1400 to a Bedfordshire family, he first saw service with King Henry V in his later French campaigns. In 1422, he was made Constable of Vernon in France and was heavily involved in the final phases of the Hundred Years War. Back in England, he became Sheriff of Bedfordshire and entered royal service. He was in the Duke of Suffolk's mission to France to negotiate peace and the hand of Margaret of Anjou. He became Queen Margaret's Chamberlain in 1445, rising through royal preferment to become a Knight of the Garter. He was wounded in 1455 at the first battle of St Albans while fighting alongside King Henry.

Soon after this event he must have reconsidered his position. Queen Margaret's letter dismissing him from his post as Chamberlain says 'Furthermore we let you weet that one of the greatest causes wherefore we discharge you is because that in this untrue troublous time ye favoured the duke of York and such as belonged to him.' He was made Speaker of the House of Commons at the first Yorkist Parliament in July 1455. In 1459 he fought for the Yorkists at Bloore Heath, and was attainted (put outside the protection of the law, with loss of all rights and forfeiture of his estates) in the same year after the episode of Ludford Bridge. He escaped to Calais with the Nevilles, returning to fight for Edward with distinction at Mortimer's Cross, Ferrybridge and Towton, following which honours were heaped upon him: Chief Butler of England, Treasurer of Ireland, Chamberlain of the Duchy of Lancaster. In 1462 he was created Baron Wenlock and made a member of the Privy Council.

He became involved with Warwick the Kingmaker through serving with him on various diplomatic missions to Europe on behalf of King Edward, and he escaped suspicion of implication in Warwick's conspiracies because he was conducting Edward's sister Elizabeth to her wedding to the Duke of Burgundy at the time. In 1469, he became Lieutenant of Calais, Warwick's deputy.

When Warwick left England in 1469 after the failure of his plot to put Clarence on the throne, Wenlock refused him entry into Calais, probably through friendship to Warwick, because of the hostile reception which was waiting for him from a garrison loyal to Edward.

He then slipped away from Calais and joined Warwick and Margaret of Anjou. His reasons for defecting were probably a sense of loyalty to Warwick and a dislike of King Edward's policies at home and in Europe.

He travelled back to England with Queen Margaret and Prince Edward to learn of the defeat at Barnet and the death of his friend Warwick. He stayed with the Lancastrians on the campaign and at Tewkesbury he was given a key role in the centre of the army, protecting the young Prince Edward, the Lancastrian heir.

What happened in the battle is shrouded in mystery. Contemporary accounts have it that Wenlock was killed in the battle, but there is no record of his burial, either at Tewkesbury or in the family chapel at St Mary's, Luton. Edward Hall suggests that his inaction following Somerset's advance was the result of treachery, and that Somerset killed him on the spot by splitting his head open. Recent research suggests that this may have been an elaborate ruse, and that Wenlock was not killed at Tewkesbury at all, dying in London some ten years later. If this is true, it would be a surprising escape and a remarkably long life for a man so heavily involved in English state affairs in the fifteenth century.

Someries Castle, Lord Wenlock's Luton seat, built of brick under his supervision.

King Henry VI

Henry VI is not only the youngest king England has had but he is the only king ever to have been crowned in both England and France. His reign was longer than all but three of England's rulers. His piety was such that he came close to being canonised. Yet he ranks among the worst and least able of English kings, and his own ineptitude was the primary cause of the unrest which overthrew him.

Henry was born at Windsor on 6 December 1421. His father died on 31 August 1422 and Henry became king. Through the years of his minority England and France were ruled by his uncles, his father's brothers. Remarkably, Henry seemed to take an early interest in matters of state and assumed his duties and responsibilities as king when he was barely sixteen. He had grown up with strong and dominant advisors, latterly Humphrey, Duke of Gloucester and Cardinal Henry Beaufort, who accustomed Henry to the domination of his councillors which would last through his life. He had no interest in things military, and always appeared to support councillors advocating peace, which unfortunately wasn't tempered with sound judgement and reasoned argument. Even when advisors demonstrated their incompetence by their actions, Henry continued to favour them. His first independent acts as king were to reward his favourites and this became a feature of his reign. Expenditure was out of control and Henry ran up huge debts which he was not able to repay from his sources of income. He borrowed to build his two principal monuments, Eton College, founded in 1440, and King's College, Cambridge, in 1441. His chief creditor was Richard, Duke of York.

Henry VI.

His obsessive piety is often confused with lack of wits but he was well read and bilingual, so clearly had no learning difficulty. In 1437, Piero da Monte wrote that 'he avoided the sight and conversation of women, affirming these to be the work of the devil and quoting from the gospel, "he who casts his eyes on a woman so as to lust after her has already committed adultery with her in his heart".' He gained a degree of respect for his simple piety, and the failures of state were ascribed to others: Bishop Moleyns, Lord Saye and Sele and the Dukes of Suffolk and Somerset were all killed because of their positions close to the king and their actions in his name.

Henry married Margaret in 1445. He seems to have shown a genuine affection for her, but it was eight years before she provided the heir who was so badly needed. Given Henry's personality, there were numerous rumours, exaggerated by Yorkist commentators. The birth was marred by Henry's sudden and unexpected illness. Though this has been blamed on a family weakness inherited from his French grandfather, the symptoms shown by Charles VI were quite different from Henry's. He lapsed into a state of mental and physical incapacity which lasted from July 1453 to December 1454 and seems never to have fully recovered, which perhaps explains some of the strange behaviour he exhibited during the Wars of the Roses.

Henry had little impact on Lancastrian policy during the conflict. He was always a victim, the real conflict being between the affinities of Richard, Duke of York and Queen Margaret. He was wounded in the first battle of St Albans and fell into Yorkist hands. The same thing happened at the battle of Northampton. Each time he was compelled to sanction a Yorkist government. At the second battle of St Albans it is said that he was placed under a tree a mile away where he laughed and sang. In 1463 he was cast adrift in northern England, being captured two years later and confined to the Tower.

Except for a short period of freedom when the Kingmaker restored him to the throne, Henry spent the remainder of his life in the Tower. Every record of his stay there suggests that the life suited him well. On 21 May 1471, Edward IV arrived in triumph back in London, with the captive Queen Margaret. Later that day, Henry was murdered, because of who he was, not what he was. There was no great protest.

Henry's claim to the throne was through John of Gaunt.

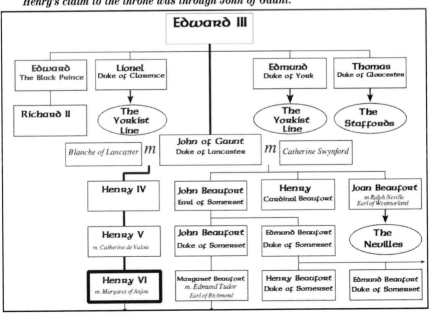

Margaret of Anjou

On 24 March 1430, Isabel, Duchess of Lorraine, wife of René, Duke of Anjou, King of Sicily, gave birth to a second daughter, Margaret. Duke René was cousin to the King of France and a descendant of Geoffrey of Anjou, father of the Plantagenet dynasty. He spent his life in the maelstrom of European power-politics, gaining and losing counties, duchies and kingdoms through inheritance, marriage and force of arms. As Margaret grew up, the Kingdom of France was being forged by Charles VII, and the English occupiers were being driven from the land.

Queen Margaret of Anjou

When Margaret entered her teens, she was an object of desire among the European nobility, encouraged by her father, who sought ever more titles and allegiances for his family. The Counts of St Pol, Charolais and Nevers sought betrothal contracts. The latter was a nephew of Philip of Burgundy. It was Frederick of Hapsburg, later elected Emperor Frederick III, to whom she was promised, however.

It is said that King Henry VI of England became besotted with her. He had heard of the fame of her beauty, and asked for some proof. He was sent a miniature portrait, and his mind was set. The Earl of Suffolk, veteran of the Siege of Orleans, was despatched to France in 1444 to negotiate. Margaret's future was clearly seen to be more secure with the real King of England than the possible Emperor of Germany, and Frederick was abandoned. The dowry negotiations were unusual for the period. Suffolk was persuaded that the Duchy of Anjou was penniless, and mortgaged to the Duke of Burgundy, as indeed it was. There would be no dowry. Worse still, Suffolk was persuaded that in exchange for the match Henry should renounce all claims to Anjou and Maine. Whilst Henry was very content with this arrangement, Suffolk must have been aware of the resentment that this would cause in England once it was known. He broke the news slowly.

On 22 April 1445 Margaret was married to Henry at Tichfield Abbey. She was plunged, at the age of fifteen, into a hotbed of intrigue in a court that was very different from that of her uncle, Charles VII. Thanks to Margaret's influence, the Duke of Suffolk rose to be Henry's favoured advisor. The agreement over Maine was very unpopular and Henry vacillated. Charles gave up on diplomacy and invaded Maine in 1448. Henry could do little to stop him and Maine fell. The French army then moved on to Normandy and to Aquitaine. In a short period England had lost all her French possessions except Calais and people saw the King's marriage contract as the catalyst. The Duke of Suffolk was impeached, banished and murdered.

Margaret did not forgive those she saw as responsible. Chief among these was Richard, Duke of York.

It might be argued that the breakdown of law and order among the nobility was in no small part due to Margaret's, rather than Henry's, policies. When fighting broke out, Margaret, not Henry, was seen as the leader of the Lancastrian party. She showed her mettle and her ruthlessness in this role to such an extent that she has been credited with the tactical decisions which led to the slaughter of the Yorkist leadership at the battle of Wakefield, despite her being hundreds of miles away at the time. Her inability to control the excesses of her army on the march south after this battle, though, lost her the war, as London was closed against her and many joined Edward, the new Duke of York, who gained the kingdom with victory at Towton. Margaret fled to France and in return for a promise to surrender Calais she was given

A modern memorial to the House of Anjou at Angers Cathedral.

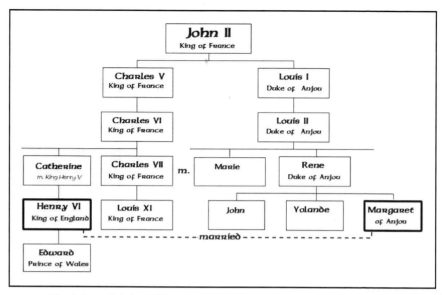

The dukes of Anjou shared ancestors with the Valois kings of France, to whom they were also related by marriage.

the means to invade England by the French king, Louis XI. The invasion was ineffectual and she found herself back in France with her young son and living in penury in Koeur Castle, near Verdun.

When Warwick the Kingmaker arrived unexpectedly in Honfleur in 1470, Louis remembered his cousin Margaret, and persuaded her to join Warwick in the adventure which culminated in the battle of Tewkesbury, a second defeat and even greater sorrow with the death of her son and her own imprisonment.

In the year 1475 the English invaded France, but rather than fight, Edward IV agreed a truce with King Louis. One of the clauses of the treaty was an agreement to ransom Margaret back to her family for 50,000 gold crowns. Margaret arrived at Dieppe in January 1476. At Rouen, she learned the cost of her freedom: Louis expected her to renounce her right of inheritance to all her father Duke René's lands of Lorraine, the Barrois, Anjou and Provence, which would now pass to the French crown. She had now lost everything. She begged a home in Angers and a pension from her father. On his death in 1480, King Louis was merciless in pursuing her for her inheritance. She wrote in desperation to one of the king's councillors:

'Monsieur de Bouchange, I commend myself to you as much as I can. The King has made known to the town of Angers that the King of Sicily, my father, is gone to God. I am writing to him that it may please him to take my poor case, in the matter of what

108

can and should belong to me, into his hands to do with it according to his good will and pleasure, and still keep me in his good grace and love, in which I pray you to be good enough to maintain me always. And I commend you to God, Monsieur de Bouchange, may he give you all that you wish. Written at Reculée-les-Angiers, the first day of August 1480.'

Louis would not listen to her pleas. He enforced their agreement to the letter, and beyond. It was only the compassion of Francis Vignolles, lord of Morains, that saved her from destitution. He offered her a home in the Castle of Dampierre, near Saumur, where she spent the rest of her life. In August 1482, she suddenly became very feeble. She died, without servants, kinless and friendless, on threadbare sheets, of old age. She was fifty-two.

Edward, Prince of Wales

The birth of an heir to the throne, particularly after eight years of childless marriage, should be a cause of great celebration in the nation. Jubilation at Prince Edward's birth, on 13 October 1453, was more restrained, though, and his passage through life was presaged by the circumstances of his birth. His father, the king, had lost his wits some months earlier and neither recognised nor understood what was happening around him. It was an uneasy introduction to the world. His mother had all the concerns of a hostile regency, in the hands of her enemy Richard, Duke of York, to deal with as well as an incapacitated husband and a young son. King Henry recovered his wits late in 1454 and despite the allegation that on being presented with young Edward he commented that he must be the son of the Holy Ghost he was clearly delighted with his son.

The political situation in England was deteriorating rapidly through Edward's early years. The culmination came in July 1460 when the Lancastrian defeat at the battle of Northampton led to his father being taken to London as a captive and Edward and his mother fleeing to Cheshire and North Wales, where they endured great hardships in raising the army which eventually confronted the Yorkists at Wakefield and St Albans. After the second battle of St Albans, the seven-year-old Edward was given the task of deciding the fate of the two knights who had been guarding his father the king,

Edward, Prince of Wales.

who was recovered after the battle. He is alleged to have said 'Let their heads be taken off'. From contemporary comments it seems clear the young Edward was obsessed with war and violence.

After defeat at Towton in 1461 he fled with his mother, spending his early youth with her in exile in France. He was tutored by the eminent lawyer and Lancastrian Sir John Fortescue and he took pride in his studies. Some insight into his state of mind is given in 1467 by the Milanese Ambassador, who wrote, 'This boy, though only thirteen years of age, already talks of nothing but cutting off of heads or making war, as if he had everything in his hands or was the god of battle or the peaceful occupant of the throne.' He seems to have been a good horseman, and well trained in the military disciplines about which he was obsessive.

In 1470 his world was again turned upside down with the arrival of the Kingmaker and an alliance to re-conquer England. As part of the agreement his mother made, he was to marry Anne Neville, the Kingmaker's younger daughter. On 25 July, the betrothal was solemnised at Angers Cathedral. Edward was seventeen, Anne fifteen. The two had never before met and came from affinities which had been taught to hate each other. The marriage was not consummated.

After much waiting, Edward took ship back to a supposedly secure Lancastrian England in April 1471 to find that his new father-in-law had been defeated and killed and the throne was back in the hands of the Yorkists. He was probably a willing and enthusiastic supporter of staying and fighting and there is some evidence that his views were listened to. The outcome was the battle of Tewkesbury, where Edward commanded the centre of the army alongside Lord Wenlock and John Langstrother. No one believes that this eighteen-year-old had the qualities of the nineteen-year-old Yorkist captain, Richard, Duke of Gloucester. Nothing is known about the thoughts or actions of Edward, Prince of Wales, Lancastrian heir, in this battle. Even his death is shrouded in myth, though there seems to be no good reason to dispute the *Arrivall's* statement that he died fleeing the field, alongside many others who were fighting for his cause.

His body lies in Tewkesbury Abbey, though the exact location is in doubt. He became a minor cult figure under the Tudors, with some evidence of pilgrimage to his tomb.

Sir Edmund Beaufort,
Duke of Somerset

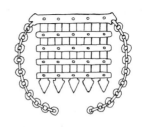

The history of the Beaufort Dukes of Somerset was short and brutal. Edmund was the fourth and last. Descendants of Edward III through John of Gaunt and Catherine Swynford, the Beauforts were constantly at the heart of matters of state. Their royal blood made them a threat to the aspirations of their Yorkist cousins.

John, the first Duke, probably committed suicide in 1444 whilst on service in the French wars. His brother, Edmund, the second Duke, was King Henry's closest advisor, and became the focus of Yorkist discontent. He was killed in 1455 at the first battle of St Albans. His eldest son, Henry, became the third Duke. After the defeat at Towton, Henry continued fighting in Northumberland but made his peace with King Edward. When he rebelled again, he was attainted and his title was forfeited. He was captured after the battle of Hexham and executed, leaving the claim to the title to his brother Edmund, always referred to in Yorkist documents as 'calling himself Duke of Somerset'.

Born in 1439, Edmund Beaufort was the second of three sons. He was arrested in 1460 by Warwick the Kingmaker and imprisoned, initially in Calais and later in the Tower. When his brother Henry was reconciled with the Yorkists Edmund was pardoned and released. He immediately fled to France and with his younger brother John he joined Queen Margaret at Koeur Castle. In January 1465 he was deprived of his title and property by a Yorkist Act of Attainder, seven months after the execution of his elder brother, the third Duke.

He joined the Duke of Burgundy with other Lancastrian exiles and fought with his army. With the marriage between Duke Charles of Burgundy and Elizabeth of York in 1468 there was a re-alignment of affinities in France. Edmund and his brother left Bruges on the day before Elizabeth, the new Duchess, arrived there. Duke Charles' sympathies were not particularly strong, and until he learned of the agreement between Warwick the Kingmaker and King Louis of France to declare war on Burgundy in return for French support to the Lancastrian cause, he was happy to see King Henry restored to the throne.

Edmund had no love for the Kingmaker, did not trust him and would have nothing to do with his campaigning. He returned to

England and was probably in the West Country in discussions with Jasper Tudor whilst the Kingmaker was restoring Henry. He played no part in the battle of Barnet, despite Hall's Chronicle saying that he commanded the main battle. He met Queen Margaret at Cerne Abbey with Sir John Courtenay, Earl of Devonshire, and probably put the case strongly for Margaret and her son to stay and fight rather than return to France.

At Tewkesbury, Edmund Beaufort was given command of the Lancastrian army. His competence is difficult to judge because of the misinformation, propaganda and speculation which have surrounded his actions over the years. He is charged with irresponsibly leading a move which was unsupported by the rest of the army and which led to defeat. He is also charged with murdering Lord Wenlock, one of his own commanders, in full view of the army. It is unlikely that there will ever be enough evidence to make an objective judgement on the former; the latter is almost certainly untrue.

Edmund Beaufort is one of those believed to have sought sanctuary in Tewkesbury Abbey and to have been surrendered to King Edward. He was certainly among those tried for treason and executed. Edward's policy of removing those who could threaten his position as king put Edmund Beaufort, one of the last Lancastrians in the royal line, in a difficult position. As he had already been attainted, and he had, with others, been proclaimed a 'rebel and traitor' following the battle of Barnet, he could not have had much hope for any other outcome.

His brother John had been killed in the battle. Neither of them had married, and with them the male line of the Beauforts ended. However, their cousin Margaret had married Jasper Tudor's brother Edmund and their son Henry revived the family fortunes in 1485.

Appendix III
Sanctuary

About the confrontation in Tewkesbury Abbey, the *Arrivall* says that it had not been granted any franchise for any offenders against their prince having recourse there. This must have been quite a tense situation, bringing the temporal power of the king and the spiritual power of the Pope into direct conflict and both sides must have been anxious to find a solution to satisfy their honour.

Sanctuary sprang from the belief that anyone within a church was under God's protection and a violator of that protection would feel God's retribution. What became a right under common practice was abused by the underclass, who used churches as convenient bases for their wrongdoing. Church and state combined to try to limit such abuses. In the time of Edward II, felons in sanctuary were required to confess their crime and take an oath that they would leave the realm, having been given safe conduct to a named seaport, a period of time to get there and a route to follow strictly. The Church had special provisions. Priests were not obliged to leave sanctuary and those who offended against the Church could be removed from sanctuary for the Church to punish.

The North of England has the best known sanctuaries: Hexham, Durham and Beverley. Beverley was viewed as the safest of all. Though every consecrated place was a sanctuary, the penalties for forced removal varied greatly. Westminster was a convenient bolt-hole for nobility in fear of their lives. The Countess of Warwick sought refuge at Beaulieu Abbey on hearing of the death of her husband. Here lay a key reason for tolerating the custom. They provided refuge for the nobility in times of trouble and it is possibly this self-interest which led to a plea for its abolition by John of Gaunt and Wyclif to be refused.

During the Cade rebellion of 1450, one of the leaders fled to the church of St Martin-le-Grand. The king demanded of the dean that he produce the traitor. The dean refused and produced his charters, which were found to give protection to the fugitive. Henry VII seems to have taken a harder line, perhaps remembering Tewkesbury. He deemed the sanctuary at Colnham, near Abingdon, to be insufficient for traitors. Several political refugees were seized and at least one of them was executed.

Though the privilege was abolished by James I, the rights lingered on and had to be re-abolished in 1697. The memory of sanctuary remains and there is even today an obvious reluctance on the part of the state to enter into places of religion if the fugitive is seen as a refugee in the modern sense.

Appendix IV

The Armies, Arms and Tactics

There is no good record of the numbers of men who fought in the battle of Tewkesbury or any other battle of the period. Accuracy with figures was not something for which the fifteenth century was noted. Roman numerals were used for recording numbers, which made errors more likely and calculation almost impossible. The *Arrivall* says that more than 3,000 Yorkist footmen travelled through the Cotswolds. After the battle, 3,436 archers were paid. This gives some clues, and the general consensus is that the Yorkist army contained between 5,000 and 6,000 men. The Lancastrian army is generally held to be a little larger, though whether this was the case or whether it is the propaganda of the winners, who would never admit to overcoming a vastly inferior army, it is not certain. Commentators accept that the Lancastrians had maybe 500 more men than the Yorkists.

The mustering of troops for a battle was achieved through a system of protectionism described as 'bastard feudalism'. Nobles maintained households which included some professional soldiers, to act as bodyguards, and others trained or being trained in arms who could be called upon to fight if required. King Edward had limited the numbers of men permitted in a household, acknowledging his need to manage over-mighty subjects. In addition to the household, noblemen had their 'affinities', lesser lords who looked to them for protection and in return would be expected to support them with troops from among their own tenants. Sometimes these lords were contracted as indentured retainers. Often the arrangements were less formal. This was an age when private quarrels could still turn into private battles, as between the Duke of Norfolk and Sir John

Right: *Mounted knight of the Wars of the Roses. This image of man and horse, clad in the finest German plate protection, represents the highest achievement of the craft of the armour maker. Apart from the head armour, it is unlikely that the horses engaged in the fighting at Tewkesbury would have been so heavily protected.*

Paston at Caister Castle in 1469, or Lord Berkeley and Lord Lisle at Nibley Green in 1470, the protagonists calling on their affinities to provide men to fight on their behalf. Such affinities were the major source of troops for Tewkesbury. Commissions of Array were also issued, in the royal name, to muster fighting men from the counties. These arrays were strictly intended to deal with foreign threats, and at a time when the royal power was weak and loyalty divided these commissions do not seem to have made a significant contribution of men to either cause. The loyalty of the local lord was the deciding factor.

The bow remained the most potent of weapons in the English armoury despite the advances in artillery and protective armour which had occurred since the heady days of the total supremacy of the English archer in fourteenth-century France. More than half of the troops would be longbowmen. These would have been of the lower class, trained with the bow from an early age by weekly practice at the butts. Longbowmen could shoot up to twelve arrows in a minute with a range of up to 300 yards. At 100 yards they were lethally accurate. Their use is recorded in the *Arrivall*, where it is said that 'the King's vanward, Richard Duke of Gloucester sore oppressed the Lancastrians with shot of arrows.'

Bows were a well-developed technology. Manufacture was undertaken in England from staves of yew often imported from the Mediterranean countries where the climate produced straighter and stronger wood. Successive kings required yew staves to be imported with other goods, particularly wine, almost as a tax. In 1472, Edward set the tariff at four staves per ton weight of merchandise, the quality being checked and certified by examining experts. Importing unfinished staves retained the knowledge of the mysteries of bow making within the kingdom. The technology of arrows, and particularly arrow heads, was the area which had to develop to match

The chain-mail piercing bodkin and other 'specialist' arrowheads.

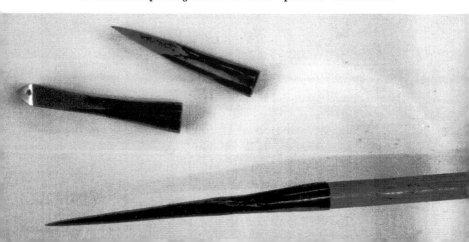

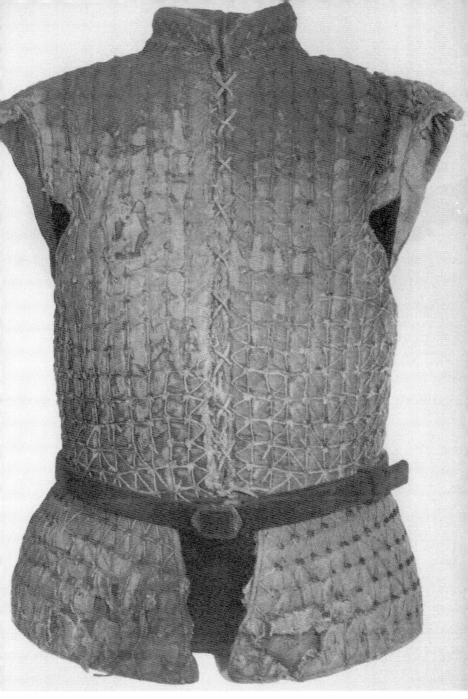

The jack. Light and practical, these were made of layers of canvas, padded and reinforced.

A fifteenth-century sallet, a simple foot soldier's head protection, possibly German. Malbork Castle, Poland

the skills of the armourer in producing 'arrow-proof' designs. Arrows were produced in their thousands, of any straight-grained timber. Those recovered from the *Mary Rose* are made of poplar, though this was considered to be an inferior wood. Ash was preferred because the arrows flew fast but had enough weight to drive the head into the target and 'delivereth a great stripe withall'. The only good fletching was the goose feather and the art of the fletcher was in matching the feather to the shaft. It was this which determined if it flew fast or slow, far or close. At the other end of the shaft was the arrow head, forged of iron, sometimes strengthened with steel. The head had to provide weight to balance the flight and to penetrate the target. If the target was the flesh of an animal, including war horses, then the head was broad and sharp. If it were a man encased in mail and plate armour then the long, narrow, pointed bodkin heads were used to penetrate links and small gaps or to punch through plate.

Archers outnumbered other classes of soldiers in late medieval battles, with ratios of between three and seven to one being quoted. They were lightly armed and normally protected only by a padded jacket and a helmet. In battle, they protected their positions from direct assault by the use of sharpened staves driven into the ground. Each archer would have two dozen or so arrows and would rely upon a supply chain from the baggage carts to replace them as he shot them. The type of arrow used would depend upon the purpose and the local captains would be charged with instructing on this. At Tewkesbury, the tactics seem to have been straightforward when compared with many other battles. Once the battle progressed to close quarters, the value of the bow was gone and the archer resorted to his arming sword or falchion, and used his lightness and wits to stay out of harm's way. How successful he was at this, or indeed if he fought or ran, is not recorded. Against a knight brought down from a horse, an archer would have an immediate advantage and access to probe into unprotected places.

In 1453 at the battle of Castillon the English army was defeated by a French force which included 700 gunners, bringing the Hundred Years War to an end. In 1470 Thomas Talbot, Lord Lisle, challenged William, Lord Berkeley to battle, writing 'I marvel that you come not forth with all your carts of guns, bows and other ordnance.' The gun was thus clearly seen by now as a weapon which had come of age, with accuracy and portability enough to challenge the supremacy of the longbow, though it would be a long time before it totally supplanted it. Because of the success of the longbow the English were late to this new weapon and looked to the German states and Flanders for gunners and the technology of guns. According to Warkworth's Chronicle, Edward's army included 300 Flemish hand-gunners provided by the Duke of Burgundy. *The Great Chronicle of London* says that Edward was accompanied by 'black and smoky sort of gunners, Flemings to the number of five hundred' on his march

A fifteenth-century gun barrel on a reconstructed carriage. Malbork Castle, Poland

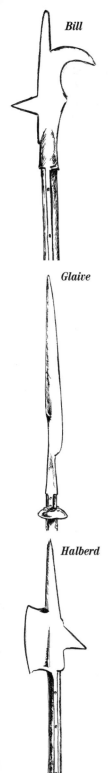

Bill

Glaive

Halberd

into London before the battle of Barnet. Warkworth also records that Margaret's return was accompanied by Frenchmen. He does not record their skills, but they were likely to have included gunners.

Hand-gunners used a simple muzzle-loading iron tube, with a rudimentary stock of iron or wood and often a monopod foot to give some stability when firing the charge. Such guns fired lead balls, up to about 20mm diameter, of the type found on the Gastons during an archaeological survey in 1997. Because the guns were slow to reload the gunners needed some protection. Close to the front line, they would duck behind large wooden shields known as paveses.

Guns existed in a wide range of sizes, from 'Mons Meg', the bombard still to be seen at Edinburgh Castle, with a bore of nearly 20 inches and capable of firing shot for two miles, to the much more portable culverins and serpentines which were mounted on carriages and could be dragged along with the army. These guns shot roughly shaped stone balls (see page 131).

The gunners lived apart from the rest of the army because of the danger involved in handling black powder and also because of the anti-social effects which constant exposure to the powder had on their digestive systems.

Infantrymen, billmen, were the next most numerous class of soldiers. Armed with long pole arms evolved from farm implements, they fought in groups, bill blocks, which could be very effective at close quarters. Some forty or fifty years later the bill would be replaced by the long pike, which was being refined as a weapon in the Swiss cantons and would soon sweep the world before it, used by men standing shoulder to shoulder, and drilled to act in absolute unison. Wars of the Roses billmen were men of peasant stock like the archers. Typically, these men were protected by a jack and sallet, and such plate armour as they could obtain. The jack was a padded, stuffed or many-layered coat sometimes reinforced with metal or horn plates and sometimes with leather. These coats were comparatively light and serviceable and their laminated construction, with up to thirty layers of cloth, was reasonable proof against arrows and swords. Sallets, helmets, came in many shapes and there was no standardisation at all. Men who did not have a metal helmet might have one of boiled leather, or of basketwork covered in leather and reinforced by iron strips. In a hastily gathered army there would probably be proportionately more men 'able with a staff' pressed into service as billmen than archers, who seem not to have been practising as they needed to, despite Acts of Parliament banning football and demanding weekly practice at the butts.

Their weapons were fitted to six-foot shafts and came in wide varieties, but all with a point for thrusting, a blade for hacking and a hook for pulling opponents over. The common forms of these weapons were bills (a favourite of the English), halberds and glaives. Their primary purpose was as thrusting weapons; while the men in the block advanced and worked together they formed a unit which would be very difficult to penetrate and break at close quarters. When two blocks met, it must have been a brave or foolhardy man who would make the first move forward into the range of the thicket of jabbing steel points. These men and weapons were the backbone of the close-quarters fighting, protecting their lords and their banners and exploiting any weaknesses in the enemy lines.

The elite of the army were the men-at-arms: noblemen, knights and esquires. These were the officers of the army, the men who lived by the chivalric code and the men who were encased in plate armour. Men of the upper classes and men like the Pastons who were aspiring to the upper classes, entered a life which revolved around the courts of the nobility and the practice of the manly skills of feats of arms and hunting. Young men were often placed in noble households to be taught the skills of a knight; first as a page, becoming an esquire in their early teens and a knight by the age of twenty-one if they merited it. An esquire would ride to war, and if he had the competence he would be expected to fight alongside the other men-at-arms.

At the battle of Tewkesbury it is likely that most men-at-arms rode to the battlefield but fought on foot. The usefulness of horses had been limited by advances in archery, guns and the formidable hedgehogs presented by billmen. The armour worn on horseback was also used on foot. This was the age of the ultimate development of armour, before the widespread use of guns rendered it pointless and by the seventeenth-century it had reduced to helmet and breastplate. The style-setters were in northern Italy, which produced armour with smooth and clean lines, and southern Germany, whose armour was heavily decorated with fluted surfaces and spiky outline. These regions produced industrial quantities of equipment, including the very best for the greatest lords. Armour was also produced more locally, in France and Flanders, adapting Italian and German styles to local tastes.

A full suit of armour, a 'harness', contains many individual parts and has to be put on very methodically with the help of an assistant. Armour is not excessively heavy and a knight is relatively mobile inside it. The two great disadvantages are the heat which is generated because of the lack of ventilation and the greatly impaired visibility, particularly when using a visor. Each piece is carefully shaped and crafted to reduce the opportunities for a probing point, from sword, bill or arrow, to find a way through a joint, and to deflect weapon blows away from vital parts of the body.

The weapon of choice for men-at-arms was the poleaxe, or battleaxe. This was a short four-foot, shafted weapon, with a head consisting of a long and stiff spike, an axe blade and a hammerhead. The other end of the shaft terminated with a metal spike. It was with a weapon such as this that Edmund Beaufort was said to have slain Lord Wenlock. The origin of the name is not from the pole used for the shaft, but from 'poll' meaning 'head', as in poll tax.

Men-at-arms were also armed with swords, the weapons of gentlemen, and daggers. Sword making was a great skill, and swords were treated with respect bordering on reverence. Fifteenth-century armour was so strong as to make shields superfluous, leaving two hands free to wield weapons. The most popular sword was the 'hand and a half', with a long well-balanced hilt and a blade with both a thrusting point and a cutting edge. These were carried in scabbards suspended from the belt.

These men were the officers of the army. There were no fixed ranks; all were 'Captains'. There was a great mixture of men: hardened and experienced soldiers, and high-born, inexperienced youths. It

Richard Beauchamp, father-in-law of Warwick the Kingmaker, clad in Italian armour in a style current in 1471.

Right: *sword, daggers, poleaxe and mace. The cutting, thrusting and crushing weapons used in close combat.*

took skill on the part of the army's commanders to keep the peace and ensure that all were working for the common goal.

English armies almost always organised themselves into three divisions, 'wards' or 'battles'. Each would be under the command of an experienced captain. The divisions marched in line, with vanward leading and rearward at the back. In battle, they would normally form a line abreast, with the van taking the right flank and the rear the left. There were, of course, numerous variations on this dictated by circumstances. The Yorkist van at Tewkesbury was on the left, for instance. Often there would be a reserve held back for tactical reasons, or a party charged with setting an ambush as at Tewkesbury.

Information about the formation of armies in the field is very scarce and almost all we know is informed conjecture. It is generally believed that archers, the biggest group of men, were positioned on either side of the division, protected from attack by sharpened stakes driven into the ground. This positioning was to allow free movement for the billmen and men-at-arms and also to give a more effective shooting line on an advancing enemy, allowing them to cover the whole front of the line whilst keeping clear of entanglement with their own infantry.

The sound and confusion of battle were overwhelming to the senses, and maintaining discipline and command was the key to victory. The commander of the army and his captains had at once to motivate their men by example, leading from the front, and to maintain a strategic overview of the unfolding battle, particularly to take advantage of any small weakness which the enemy might reveal. To do this successfully took a particular sort of talent.

Men were charged with maintaining an overview of the battle from a high point to the rear and there would be a constant stream of messengers, scurriers, taking information between them and the field command. Sending commands rapidly through the army was achieved generally by the use of trumpets and flags which used pre-agreed signals understood by those for whom they were intended.

Recognition was also a problem in the heat of the battle. With men drawn from so many places and so quickly there was no opportunity for a common uniform and men had to rely on recognising banners, badges and colours and remembering which side they represented. Sometimes mistakes had considerable consequences. At the battle of Barnet, the Lancastrians mistook the Earl of Oxford's star with streamers emblem for the Yorkist sun in splendour and attacked his forces. This probably lost them the battle and the war. The natural assumption when attacked by part of your own side was that they had defected to the enemy, so correcting mistakes was not easy.

Men of rank were recognised in battle by their banners, bearing their coat-of-arms. These were carried by banner-bearers, who remained close to their lord through the battle and were protected by the lord's bodyguard. Long, tapered flags, standards, were used as rallying points and for signalling. Standards bore the badges of a noble or knight banneret and these badges were reflected in badges worn by the men.

Household troops would be well provided with livery jackets or surcoats in the chosen colours of their lord. They would also wear badges embroidered onto patches and sewn onto their jackets. These badges were favourite devices of the nobility, sometimes taken from their heraldry but more often from personal favourites arising from superstition or a pun on their name. If time and resources permitted, badges would be issued to all who fought under their banner to allow recognition on the battlefield. These badges were much better known through the

At the battle of Barnet confusion was caused when the Lancastrian Duke of Oxford's star was mistaken for the Yorkist sun.

land than coats-of-arms and the nobility were often known by their badges. Queen Margaret's marguerite, Prince Edward's white swan, King Edward's sun in splendour and particularly Richard, Duke of Gloucester's white boar were, and are, easily recognised badges.

Banners are hung in Tewkesbury's streets every summer. This shows Richard, Duke of Gloucester's white boar badge. David Luitweiler

Appendix V
Evidence for the Battle

Interpretation of events which took place more than five hundred years ago will never be an exact science. Facts fade very quickly in human memory and stories change with the retelling. If our descendents half a millennium from now were to try to build a picture of the Second World War based entirely on the study of Allied war films there would be little likelihood of an accurate picture emerging. Our task is not dissimilar.

There are four major areas of study to aid understanding: the archaeology, the landscape, the documents and experimental re-creation.

Commentators have used combinations of these over the years to understand the battle and have come to very different conclusions. None is likely to be wholly correct. None can be dismissed out of hand.

Tewkesbury has the advantage of contemporary documents describing the battle or referring to the battle. The chronicle from the abbey, though sparse in detail, can be said to be unbiased but the *Arrivall* was written by a Yorkist who was present at the battle. Though an eyewitness account has great value, it will also contain a great deal of bias. Other commentators, both contemporary and later, were also writing for a particular audience, and commentary became shameless propaganda under the Tudors. Interest in late medieval warfare waned considerably through the seventeenth century. Antiquarians of the Hanoverian and Victorian eras reawakened interest but so much had been destroyed through the Reformation, the Civil War and people simply discarding old things that study owed much more to speculation than fact. Today, we have the advantage of the work done in transcribing and translating documents and the ongoing study and indexing of the host of wills and deeds contained in libraries and museums all over the world.

Archaeological Evidence for the Battle

Archaeology is perhaps the least useful tool for interpretation of Tewkesbury. The transient nature of the battle means that there were no permanent or even semi-permanent structures to leave traces in the ground. The battlefield covered a very wide area. Much of the core, the Gaston, was developed in the nineteenth century, with no

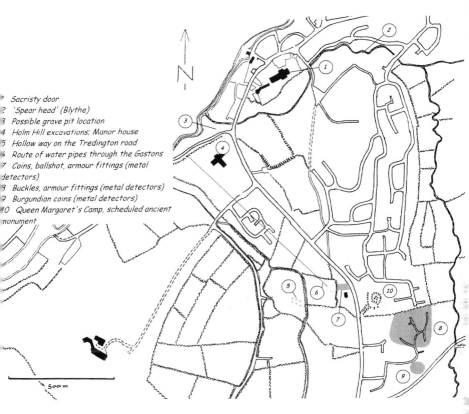

500 m

Sites and finds related to the battle.

investigation or recording. Recent developments have been preceded by field walking and included watching briefs by archaeologists, but these have revealed nothing either. The undeveloped core areas, the remaining two Gaston enclosures and the Bloody Meadow, have been subject to significant disturbance over a long period and have been trenched for sewers, an oil pipeline and the major water pipelines serving Cheltenham and Gloucester from the waterworks at Tewkesbury. As part of the work preceding the proposed development of the remaining Gaston fields in 1997 an archaeological survey was commissioned from Cotswold Archaeological Trust. Their metal detector survey revealed very little. Close to the Southwick brook they found a single lead shot, approximately 12mm in diameter, slightly flattened on one side. This may be medieval and military, though such shot was also used in the post-medieval period. They also found four possible knife blades and a horseshoe fragment which may be medieval, but the probability is that they are unrelated to the battle.

127

Because the battlefield was so close to the town, scavenging, which would have been a natural conclusion to the battle at a time when artefacts were hard won and valuable, must have been very thorough. Even today Tewkesbury abounds with rumours of finds. Every resident seems to know someone who found old swords and daggers but none of these tales is supported by hard evidence. In his account of the battle published in 1961, Lieutenant-Colonel J. D. Blythe quotes a second-hand account dating from before 1857 of a Mr Trotman finding a long piece of iron which appeared to have been part of a sword blade, and a cannonball weighing one pound six ounces. Both had been found in the Bloody Meadow. The same account refers to human bones having been discovered in the immediate neighbourhood of Gupshill. He goes on to quote an elderly man whom he talked to in 1933 who said that when he was a boy rusty knives or daggers were occasionally turned up in the Bloody Meadow. These tales are simply folk memories which reflect local belief about what may have happened. They are without any foundation whatsoever, and neither locations nor artefacts can be relied on.

Of other more substantial finds, there are some tantalising clues. Local historian Brian Linnell cites a halberd found in 1903 and sold at Christie's for six and a half guineas, and two other items, an arrow head and a spear head found during earth-moving in 1968. He also refers to an 'extensive dig' during the 1930s, the finds from which are unknown. Christie's have no record of the halberd, though the *Tewkesbury Record* reported the sale. The spear head referred to is in Cheltenham Museum. It was found on Holm Hill, and is undoubtedly a 'type 10' arrow head and associated with the extensive find of thirteenth-century arrow heads made during a major excavation on the same site in 1975, reported in the 1997 Transactions of the Bristol and Gloucestershire Archaeological Society. Lieutenant-Colonel Blythe refers to a spear head in the Tewkesbury Abbey Museum which was found in the Swilgate to the south of the abbey. This had a tang rather than a socket, which suggests that it wasn't a fifteenth-century weapon of war. None of these items has been subjected to the rigours of proper investigation and none can be linked to the battle with any confidence.

Made of limestone, this gun stone was found on the Yorkist front line. If genuine, it was dropped and abandoned because it shows no signs of having been fired.

More recently, a stone cannonball, a gun stone, was turned up by ploughing in a field south of Gupshill. Made of limestone, this appears to be genuine and is certainly of similar size and quality of manufacture to others which can be positively dated because of the context in which they were found, such as those found in the medieval ship in Newport, Gwent, in 2002.

Metal detection seems to have revealed some finds, but these are difficult to substantiate, because of the nature of the hobby. Metal detection scans have been carried out in several areas of the battlefield, apart from the work done in the Gastons by the Cotswold Archaeological Trust. Much of the scanning has been in the area of the 'Stonehills' estate prior to its development. Finds have included many fifteenth-century items. Among them are large ball shot, similar to that found in the Gastons, buckles and pieces of horse harness. Among coins found were some of Charles the Bold, Duke of Burgundy and King Edward's brother-in-law. As the area scanned included the route of the old road from the Cheltenham direction followed by the Yorkists, this could be significant. It is also possible, though, that the items could relate to others travelling the road and be nothing to do with the battle. Wool was king in the fifteenth century, Tewkesbury Abbey was heavily involved in sheep rearing and Burgundian Flanders was England's major trading partner.

The most famed relic of the battle is the armour which was beaten into long flat strips and used to reinforce the sacristy door in the abbey. Close examination of these strips does not really support this, though. It is difficult to see how a heavily shaped and irregular item of armour could have been converted into very regular rectangular plates unless there was significant re-working. Given the value

Detail of sacristy door.

Door of Tewkesbury Abbey sacristy reinforced with strips of iron reputedly beaten from scavenged armour.

of even old and unfashionable armour it seems more likely that the abbot would have traded it for purpose-made plating if it came into his possession.

Grave pits are the evidence of battles which would offer the best clues to location. There is only one reference to grave pits, other than the human bones found at Gupshill referred to above. In volume II, 1877, of the Transactions of the Bristol and Gloucestershire Archaeological Society, there is a paper on tombs in Tewkesbury Abbey by Mr S. Simonds. This says:

'With regard to the burial place of those slain in battle, it appears to have been near the old turnpike site, on the right hand side of the road to the ferry at the Lower Lode, for, during some sewerage excavations, a pit was discovered filled with human bones.'

There is no better information and no clue as to the fate of the bones. Though they would presumably have been re-interred in the town cemetery there is nothing in the burial records. The location of the sewerage excavations, which probably took place soon after 1865, is straightforward to locate. The road from Holm Bridge, up Holm Hill is part of the turnpike. Before it was built, the main road was Lower Lode Lane. There are still a sewerage pumping station and catchment pits on Lower Lode Lane, close to the junction. Immediately behind them is the Swilgate River and close by is its junction with the Mill Avon. The *Arrivall* says that 'at a mylene, in the meadow fast by the town, were many drowned'. The Mill Avon is a mill stream; the huge expanse of the Severn Ham is a notable meadow. It seems likely that men driven back to the rivers tried to cross to the town and the Ham. Their bodies, dragged from the rivers could well have been interred here. That this was the only grave pit seems unlikely. Land so close to the town and the river are not obvious choices, particularly when much of the slaughter took place at some distance, in the deer park and other places.

The fate of those buried in Tewkesbury Abbey is better recorded, though there are many uncertainties and little physical evidence within the abbey of the presence of these men. There are several lists of names associated with the battle, most of which have been transcribed from earlier sources. The *Tewkesbury Chronicle* comes to us in this form; transcribed by John Stow in the sixteenth century, it contains a detailed list of Lancastrian notables killed or executed, and details of their burial. This was examined in detail by Mr G. Rushworth in 1925. His conclusions were published in the

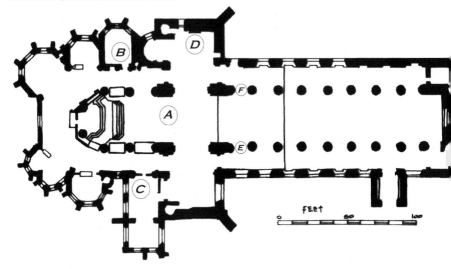

A: Memorial to Edward Prince of Wales, with 'Sun in Splendour' above
B: The Sacristy, door lined with strips of iron
C: Graves of Edmund & John Beaufort, John Courtnay, Sir T Tresham and Sir H Audley
D: Memorial to Edward, Prince of Wales
E: Graves of Sir Hampden, Sir R Wittingham, Sir J Lewknor & Sir W Vaux
F: Graves of Sir J Delves & his son and Mr H Baron

Tewkesbury Abbey plan showing sites related to the battle.

Transactions of the Bristol and Gloucestershire Archaeological Society. The Duke of Somerset was buried before an image of St James at an altar in the monastery church on the north side. His brother John, Marquis of Dorset, and cousin of Sir John Courtenay, Earl of Devonshire, are both recorded as being buried at the same altar. This altar, swept away at the Reformation, was in a chapel which is now the abbey shop. The Reformation also ended the 'daily mass in the chapel of St James the Apostle for the souls of Prince Edward, only son of King Henry VI, Edmund Earl of Richmond, the King's father, Edmund Duke of Somerset and John his brother, who were buried in the monastery'. This was ordered by Henry Tudor after taking the throne as King Henry VII. There is a memorial tablet to the Courtenay dead below the window in front of which the altar once stood (unfortunately now hidden behind the shop display cases). This is a twentieth-century work. Though not contemporary with the battle, there are two others interred in the abbey: Isabel, eldest daughter of Warwick the Kingmaker, and her husband George, Duke of Clarence, brother of King Edward. Tewkesbury was in their possession, as lord of the manor, and they chose to be buried there after their deaths in 1477 and 1478 respectively. There are no other memorials except those for the prince.

There are conflicting accounts of the fate of Prince Edward's remains. The Chronicle referred to above has him buried in the choir but there is an old and persistent belief, probably fuelled by Tudor propaganda, that he was buried with the common men. James Bennett, writing in the early nineteenth century, is also in doubt. There was a large marble slab with brasses at the entrance to the choir which was believed to be Edward's tomb. This was torn out and discarded during alterations at the end of the eighteenth century.

In a seventeenth-century book, *An Historie from Marble*, Thomas Dingley describes the tomb in some detail, as of grey marble 'the brass whereof hath bin pickt out by sacrilegious hands'. He says that it is directly

This detail of Prince Edward's tombstone is copied from Dingley's 1660 sketch. It suggests a figure in a long gown, a typical funerary image for royalty.

underneath the tower, at the entrance into the quire. This was the monk's quire, which was in front of the current choir. During the alterations, in 1796 the bones of a youth were found by the pulpitum step at the west entrance to the monk's quire. A brass memorial plate was put under the tower by the vicar, the Reverend Robert Knight.

Further alterations were made in the 1870s, during which the tomb of Henry Beauchamp, Duke of Warwick, was excavated in the chancel and a grave was found by the north west pier of the tower with a coffin which had part of the Prince of Wales', helm carved on

The sun in splendour. King Edward's badge is displayed on the sanctuary ceiling, above the Lancastrian heir's memorial.

A plaque for Edward, Prince of Wales, set into the floor of the sanctuary at Tewkesbury Abbey.

it. These alterations involved re-laying the chancel floor and inserting a diamond-shaped brass memorial plate with a text by J.D.T. Niblett. The earlier memorial was moved to the south transept.

Both plaques have Latin texts. The earlier one translates as:

'That the memory of Edward Prince of Wales, brutally murdered after the battle fought in the fields close by, perish not utterly, the piety of the people of Tewkesbury had this memorial laid down in 1796.'

The inscription on the later plaque is not quite as judgemental. It reads:

'Here lies Edward, Prince of Wales, cruelly slain whilst but a youth, anno Domini 1471 May 4th. Alas the savagery of men. Thou art the sole light of thy mother, the last hope of thy race.'

Above this memorial to the last Lancastrian there is a beautifully decorated and gilded Yorkist sun in splendour emblem on the choir ceiling. This juxtaposition presents a powerful image of the drama of events at the end of the Middle Ages.

Landscape Evidence for the Battle

There is very little of the fifteenth-century landscape which would be recognisable today. Almost everything about the way we use and manage land has changed and clues to how it used to be have to be sought in all sorts of places. Physical features are the most stable indicators. Building work, levelling, landscaping and the ubiquitous landfill have eaten away some features but have not affected the major contours. Agricultural use can be hypothesised from place and field names, field boundaries, remnants of ridge-and-furrow, crop marks and old documents, which often describe landscape in some detail. Roads become a little more difficult. Concepts of transport have changed in five hundred years and our modern idea about what constitutes a road or a path differs greatly from the medieval, where priorities were very different. In a world where wheeled traffic was very much an exception, where man and beast moved on foot, journeys were seasonal, travel to the next parish was a notable event for most and travellers were looked upon with huge suspicion, there was no pressure for anything more than keeping bridges in repair. Of all the lost landscape features, though, water is the one most difficult to understand. Field drainage was achieved through the furrows between the ridges, if at all. Wetlands abounded. Rivers had not been controlled by weirs and their reaction to the weather was more instant and dramatic than now. In wet weather they flooded

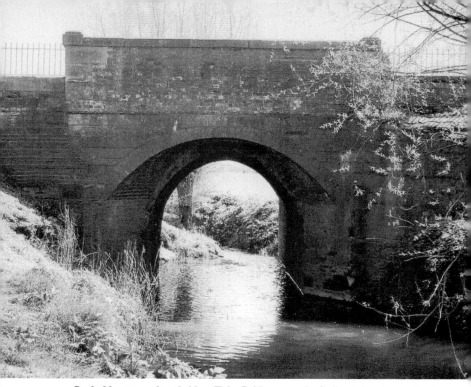

Probably once a drawbridge, Holm Bridge, over the Swilgate has been raised and widened many times.

uncontrollably. In dry weather even major rivers slowed to a muddy trickle. Because drainage is now so highly developed and because rivers are now managed by weirs and buffer reservoirs, it is hard to model how it used to be.

Tewkesbury lies on a flood plain and suffers regular winter inundations from the waters of the Severn and Avon rivers and the tidal effects of the Severn estuary. This is the dominant feature of the area, guiding both settlement and land use. The town grew up on a small area of higher ground, which frequent flooding turned into an island until causeways raised the roads above the common flood levels. This was in comparatively recent times. Agriculturally, society was close to self-sufficiency. Ownership of strips in open fields and grazing rights on common land provided what most families needed for sufficiency. The lord and the abbey generated surplus of stock and wool which were traded to Gloucester, or further afield in the case of wool. Others bartered for their needs with their peers or the small merchant community in the town. The need for roads was small, except to take them to their land, or to move stock from summer to winter pastures.

The crossing point at Lower Lode has not moved and the modern Lower Lode Lane was probably the major summertime route from the town, either to Gloucester via the riverbank or over the river into Malvern Chase and thence to Wales. The route to Gloucester would have been broad and ill defined along the riverside meadows. In some places the flood plain is narrowed because of the underlying geology, as at Sandhurst. In others there are tributary streams to cross, such as the River Chelt. Willow and alder would have abounded, some managed and harvested, but much simply growing wild on the banks. Much of the army must have abandoned the banks, because of the difficulty of dragging carts and heavy equipment over soft and boggy ground. Their routes would have been through the Severn terraces and the roads between the villages: '... a foul country, all in lanes and stony ways, betwixt woods, without any good refreshing' (the

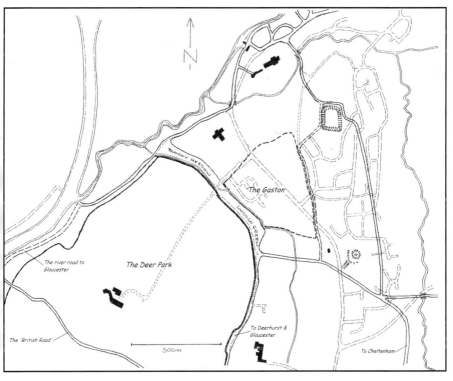

Routes of roads and paths south of Tewkesbury at the time of the battle remain uncertain. Those shown here are to a large extent speculative. Present roads are shown as dashed lines.

137

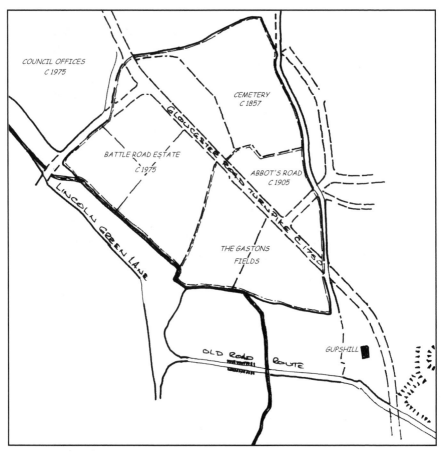

The Gaston Field. Over the years it has been enclosed and developed leaving only two open fields, 'the Gastons'.

Arrivall). At the town end of the road, the bridging point over the Swilgate, the modern Holm Bridge, has not moved. Today, the road level has been built up greatly to bring it above the flood plain. Much of this was done when the road was turnpiked by filling it with spoil taken from the cutting made up Holm Hill. The medieval bridge was perhaps six feet lower. Though there is no evidence, the bridge is likely to have been a drawbridge. Tewkesbury had no walls but it had ample moats and night-time protection against outlaws and brigands would be provided by drawbridges.

The other road south towards Gloucester passed through Lincoln Green and on towards Deerhurst. This was a higher, all-seasons route but more tortuous and more wooded. Much of it exists today as tracks and footpaths. Alongside the section to Lincoln Green is a long, narrow field, which gives every indication that it was once part of the road, wide because it is boggy and prone to flooding, and possibly also as a marshalling area for drovers. This field is a continuation of the Bloody Meadow, which leads to the possibility that these two fields formed the main route from Lower Lode Lane to Lincoln Green, and the suggestion that the route up Holm Hill was much less significant, if it existed at all. The routes from Gloucester, then, as they approached Tewkesbury, were all to the west of the battlefield.

The road used by the Yorkist army was much less direct. Though Cheltenham was referred to in the *Arrivall* it was just another village among the many on the plain below the Cotswold escarpment. The road passed from village to village and on to Tredington, the probable Yorkist campsite. Routes from Tredington ran along the meadows beside the Swilgate. The choice really depended on where it was most convenient to cross the river. As crossing was a slow and hazardous business, Edward must have opted for the bridge on the edge of Tredington rather than that on the edge of Tewkesbury. This route rises out of the river valley to pass Gupshill and join the other road at Lincoln Green. Except for a hollow way behind Gupshill, all trace of this road is now gone, though parts of it survived in use well beyond the establishment of the turnpike, and the creation of the modern A38.

Over the years, commentators on the battle and local historians have disagreed about a number of things. Leaving aside the location and conduct of the battle, most disagreement has been about the layout of roads on Tewkesbury's outskirts and the interpretation of man-made features in the landscape.

In understanding the battle, the road layout is not particularly relevant. The routes described above are not in question, at least not in the areas with which we are concerned. The size and location of the Gaston field is defined even today by field and curtilage boundaries. The path from the Gander Lane bridge passes along one of these boundaries towards Gupshill, so we can be fairly certain about that. Beyond the Swilgate is the Rudgeway, an ancient route skirting Tewkesbury and passing close to Tredington. This was of no value to Edward as it runs on the wrong side of the river.

The fields over which the battle was fought will always be the subject of speculation. Two features are named in early sources. The Park cannot be other than the deer park now occupied by Tewkesbury Park Hotel's golf course. It fits in with every detail of the

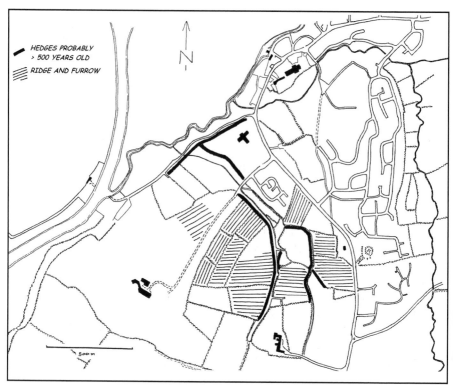

Ancient landscape features. Most of the man-made features of the fifteenth century have been swept away. This plan shows remaining hedges and ridge-and-furrow features which may be from the period.

Arrivall commentary. Gaston is referred to by Leland as the site 'entered into' by the Lancastrians. The *Arrivall* has them in a field with the town and the abbey at their backs. The Gaston was a field of about forty-one acres which in 1540 is recorded as part of the abbey estates. In 1632 it was pasture and had then been newly divided into northern and southern parts. On the 1825 map the Gaston has become seven fields, collectively 'the Gastons'. By then it had been bisected by the turnpike road and had lost its coherence. The only clue to its past is in the obvious field boundary, which remains to this day. The eastern portion was developed by the beginning of the twentieth century. The town cemetery occupied the north-east and by the time of the First World War the remainder of the eastern portion had been developed as an affluent suburb of Tewkesbury, home for solicitors, doctors and businessmen. The four western fields remained untouched until 1975, when the northern two were

140

developed for housing as part of a wider plan which saw offices built on Holm Hill and the Park, site of the old deer park, developed as an hotel and golf course.

Two enclosures of the old Gaston field remain in agricultural use. They are in the most significant part of the battlefield, and include the area which must have been defended by the Duke of Somerset. All of the landscape features described in the *Arrivall*, the hedges and dikes and the hill in a close from which Somerset mounted his attack on the King's ward, can be seen and identified from these fields. Edward Hall says that 'The Duke of Somerset, intending to abide the battle like a politic warrior, trenched his camp around about of such an altitude, and so strongly...'. This trenching would not have amounted to a great deal, given the time and resources available to do it, and nothing of it remains in the landscape. The right flank and centre of the army was protected by the hedge of the Gaston and in part by the ditch of the Southwick brook, flowing along the field boundary. Though there is a great deal of uncertainty about the field layout, it seems likely that there was a line of field hedges east of the Gaston towards the Swilgate River, which would be a convenient anchor point for the left flank. Any reinforcement carried out probably did not extend far beyond strengthening what was already there with felled timber, extending and enlarging ditches and barricading roads and paths; nothing which leaves any permanent reminder of their presence.

Medieval agriculture in central England predominantly used the 'open field' system, where crops were rotated over two or three very large fields in which villagers cultivated 'strips'. Ploughing strips is one of the causes of the ridge-and-furrow patterns common in shire counties even today. The other cause is land drainage improvement. Tewkesbury's main open field was the Oldbury, close to the town centre. Some commentators have suggested that the Gaston was a second field. At forty acres it would be large enough and the remaining parts show evidence of ridge-and-furrow. Its triangular shape would make it an unlikely common field, though, and its location on a ridge and fairly distant from settlements also tend to discount this idea. Information on land ownership is scarce but we do know that at the dissolution of the monastery it was in the ownership of the Church, as part of their Southwick estate. There is no reason to doubt that it was part of the same estate in 1471. There is plenty of evidence that the monastery was heavily involved in sheep rearing and the Gaston would be ideal pasture land. The boundaries of the

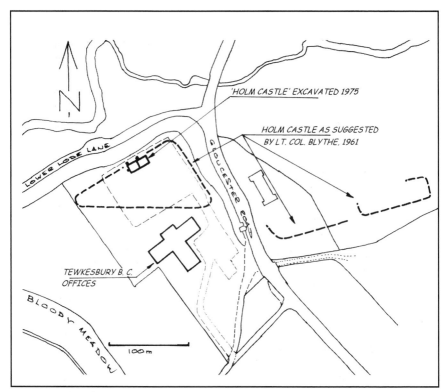

Plan of Holm Hill, showing the relationship between features real and imagined.

field are likely to have been defined by the features on the edges: the Southwick brook flows alongside the western hedge, the track to the Gander Lane bridge along the eastern and Lincoln Green Lane along the northern. Fencing the gaps between, to contain the sheep, would have been a relatively easy task. This is likely to have been the landscape the Lancastrians entered into: a grassy spring meadow contained within strong and unkempt hedges. Part of the old field hedge remains, unfortunately now without its elm trees but otherwise little changed.

Ridge-and-furrow is common in the fields south of Tewkesbury although there are no clues to earlier field systems. Medieval ridge-and-furrow has characteristics missing in this area. There is no evidence that new enclosures were made over the old field systems because there is no continuity of the patterns through field boundaries. There is no sign at all of the characteristic curve at the end of the ridge, where the ploughman started to turn his oxen as the headland at the end of the field approached. In all likelihood, the patterns seen today are the result of post-medieval field improvements, helping with land drainage rather than evidence of medieval farming practice.

Hooper's law gives a guide to the age of hedges, from the hypothesis that one new woody plant species colonises a hedge every hundred years or so. Counting the species in a run of hedge gives its age, very approximately. This technique has shown that the deer park hedge is of great antiquity, as are some of the remaining Gastons hedges and those of Lower Lode Lane and the Bloody Meadow.

Field names have been recorded in deeds and wills over the years but until recently they have not been referenced to maps. Locating fields has relied on landmarks, which have either been erased or forgotten. Local historian Brian Linnell did an invaluable service by trawling through these records and identifying the fields they refer to, using a map showing field boundaries dating from 1825. The huge majority of names relate to owners, uses or features of the fields. The Gastons is of known antiquity. The Bloody Meadow can be found as the 'Blody Furlong' in 1498, which is a remarkably fast renaming, suggestive of the effect that the slaughter there had on the townspeople. There is no record of the Knight's Field, near Gaston, where Edward had rewarded his supporters after the battle. The only other 'battle' name is Battylham, a name long disappeared. An account for sale of herbage of meadows, from 1528–9 includes the only reference to this field: '12s of Abbot of Tewkesbury for farm of seven and a half acres of meadow called le Seggelese next the bridge there and next Homecrosse alias Batylham'. Another entry refers to Homecrosse as being a meadow of one and three-quarter acres. There are clues there to place the field. Linnell associates it with the eastern slope of Holm Hill, towards the Vineyards, occupied now by Shepherd's Mead. The only uncertainty comes from the fact that 'Ham' almost invariably refers to land in the flood plain. There are no clues as to the part this site had in the battle. It is a long way from the front lines and has none of the Bloody Meadow characteristics to suggest slaughter. Could it have been the Knight's Field? It is on the battlefield, elevated to give easy visibility to an audience and close enough to the town and abbey to impress the dignity of the proceedings upon them.

A feature which has been the subject of much interest has been Holm Castle. This mythical building was well described by John Leland:

'A little above the bridge Avon breaketh into two arms, the right arm cometh into Severn within a flight shot of the bridge. The other arm cometh down by the side of the town and abbey: leaving it to the east, and so passing there hard by Holm Castle goeth into Severn.'

He also says that the location is close to where the Swilgate enters the Avon, and

'There has been in time of mind some parts of the castle standing. Now some ruins of the bottoms of the walls appear. Now it is called Holm Hill.'

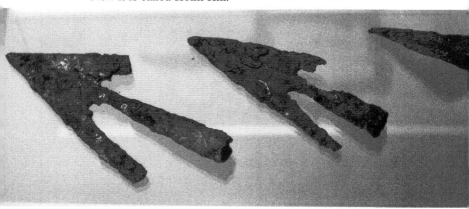

Thirteenth-century hunting arrow heads excavated on the site of 'Holm Castle'. Tewkesbury Museum

There can be little doubt that the site described is that now occupied by the Borough Council offices, a fact confirmed by an archaeological excavation which preceded the building in 1975 and which is reported in the 1997 Transactions of the Bristol and Gloucestershire Archaeological Society. This found, among other things, a manor house, of rectangular plan, about 30 metres long and 10 metres deep, which had been abandoned in the fourteenth century and much of the stone robbed out. This fits every detail of Leland's description, except for its being a castle. As the home of the powerful de Clare marcher lords, it was probably defendable but there is no evidence for gates or curtain walls. James Bennett, writing in 1830, put Holm Castle several hundred metres to the east, on the evidence of masses of stone and brick which were uncovered when the area was levelled in 1826. Bennett's version has found its way onto the obelisk erected on the Vineyards in 1932, which now purports to mark the site of a castle. The likelihood is, though, that there was a large house on that

Somerset's Charge

The view over the Yorkist lines at the hill down which Somerset's fellowship charged.

site, called Vineyard House in 1685. Levelling and re-grading in that area has altered the topography to the extent that there are no longer any clues in the landscape.

On the south of the battlefield, there were settlements at Southwick, an abbey estate, and at Gupshill. Close to Gupshill is the moated site of Queen Margaret's Camp. Although popularly associated with the Lancastrian front line, the building which occupied the site was likely to have been abandoned and destroyed by 1471. Other than as a defensive outpost for a few men, which would have no tactical advantage and would be almost a suicidal mission, there is no obvious role for it in the battle.

Close to Southwick Manor, adjacent to the extension of Lincoln Green Lane towards Deerhurst, there is a field, a close, with a very distinctive hillock within it. This lane, close and hillock are the best fit for the Duke of Somerset's action described in the *Arrivall*. If this move is taken at face value, there are some landscape issues which are hard to reconcile with the description. They are about Somerset's ability to move a significant force, unseen, past the Yorkist flank and his ability to charge down a long slope with a stream at the foot of it into the Yorkist army and still retain an element of surprise. There is, though, no better explanation.

145

Documentary Evidence for the Battle

Edward IV's campaign to regain the throne in 1471, of which the battle of Tewkesbury is a central feature, is unusual in having a detailed and well-written written account which is contemporary with the battle. Tradition has it that it is the work of one Nicholas Harpsfield, Clerk of the Signet to King Edward. The evidence for his authorship is scarce but what is certain is that it was written by someone who travelled with the Yorkists. Comments referring to the suffering of the foot soldiers at the rear of the army suggest that the writer was among them, not riding in the van with the royal party. The account comes down to us thanks to a copy made of an original manuscript in the library of William Fleetwood, Recorder of London, by the antiquarian John Stow some time in the sixteenth century. The account covers the events of the whole Yorkist campaign in considerable detail, from the landing at Ravenspur to the death of King Henry. A version edited by John Bruce was published by the Camden Society in 1838. This edition is readily available in print, or from the Internet. It has a less than memorable title, *Historie of the Arrivall of Edward IV in England and the finall recouerye of his kingdoms from Henry VI AD M.CCCC.LXXI*. It gives a thorough, if partisan, account of events and has been extensively quoted in this text, referred to as 'the *Arrivall*'.

Closely related to the *Arrivall* is the Ghent manuscript. So named because it was found and is held in the library of Ghent University, this is an account in French which seems to have been sent with a letter to the nobles and burgomasters of Bruges by King Edward to thank them for the courteous hospitality he had received from them during his exile. The account is a précis of the *Arrivall*. It is most noted for the four beautifully painted miniatures which illuminate the text, including views of the death of Prince Edward in battle and the execution of the Duke of Somerset. Unfortunately, these are clearly not accurate visual representations, so no reliance can be placed on them in interpreting events.

There are other contemporary sources which refer to the events surrounding the battle from differing perspectives. *The Paston Papers*, a collection of fifteenth-century correspondence, includes letters from the Paston sons, one of whom fought in the battle of Barnet, and other letters with considerable detail about the political and social situation. *The Great Chronicle of London* and the *Coventry Leet Book*, among others, contain references to the political and social situation of the period and, like the 'little book' from Tewkesbury

Abbey which John Leland transcribed, they give an insight into national events from a local perspective.

Other traces of the battle are more fleeting and less reliable. John Warkworth's *Chronicle of the first thirteen years of the reign of King Edward the fourth*, written within a decade or so of the events, gives a very brief account. His Lancastrian viewpoint introduces subtle pieces of information which cause disputes even today. He has the Prince of Wales calling for succour to his brother-in-law Clarence and then killed. He has the Lancastrians in the abbey being pardoned by King Edward and then executed. He has King Henry murdered and bleeding on the pavement at St Paul's. The *Crowland Chronicle* 'second continuation', probably dating from the first years of Tudor rule, also makes reference to the battle, and also presents information in a subtly different way; this time the death of Edward, Prince of Wales is described as being after the battle, reflecting a rumour that he was taken alive and murdered. This theme was developed by later Tudor writers.

There is a short document, the *Manner and Guiding of the Earl of Warwick at Angers,* which describes Warwick's stay in Angers in July 1470, where the negotiations with Louis and Margaret led to the Lancastrian invasion. This is written entirely from Warwick's viewpoint and seeks to justify his actions.

The interests of the King of France and Duke of Burgundy in the affairs of England mean that documents from their courts contain references which help interpret unfolding events, though these are not necessarily accurate in all details. Jean de Waurin, a diplomat in the service of the Dukes of Burgundy, and Philippe de Commines, who served both the Duke of Burgundy and the King of France, wrote memoirs which include information about events in England, though these are not always accurate. The Milanese State papers contain numbers of reports provided by envoys of the Dukes of Milan to England, France and Burgundy. These report a great deal of fact and rumour about the tangled affairs of the three powers.

Tudor writers put a subtly different slant on events, and in particular there was a tendency to demonise Richard, Duke of Gloucester, who as Richard III was the Yorkist king overthrown by the Tudors. To justify the usurpation, Robert Fabyan, Polydore Vergil, Edward Hall and particularly Raphael Holinshed progressively developed the myths which became the source material of Shakespeare's history plays.

John Leland wrote from a very different perspective. His mission was to save the knowledge of English history which was stored in the monastic libraries and his 'Itinerary' is a reliable source where it relates to Tewkesbury, accurately recording the origin of all that he wrote. He adds nothing to the conduct of the battle but he gives us clues about the location (being the only writer to refer to the battle of Gaston) and the landscape as it was some seventy years after the battle.

It would be wrong to say that the Middle Ages were forgotten until the twentieth century but there was certainly not the level of interest in the 'recent' past. Histories, where they were published, relied heavily on previously published work, with limited reference to primary sources or to the records of the period.

Appendix VI
A History of Accounts of the Battle

In common with many battlefields, Tewkesbury has been subject to speculation and re-interpretation over the years. The location and progress of the battle became particularly important in 1997, when English Heritage chose to test the status of its Battlefield Register at Tewkesbury by opposing a plan to build houses on the last undeveloped Gaston fields. The rival views were debated in front of a planning inspector, who decided in favour of the Battlefield Register version of events, which closely corresponds to that described in this book. In the absence of any new information, the balance of probability is with this version but there cannot be any certainty with such scant evidence.

The first 'modern' written accounts of the battle were contained in the histories of Tewkesbury produced by Dyde in 1787 and Bennett in 1830. These were local publishers and booksellers. Bennett in particular had a keen sense of history and a good grasp of events. His discussion of the battle rejects the then popular view that the Lancastrians encamped in the Vineyards, arguing that this was an unsuitable place to choose to defend and that 'we must therefore believe that the Duke of Somerset was much more deficient in the arts of war than he has ever been represented, before we can suppose he would have selected a position so objectionable'. Bennett supports the site of 'History, tradition and probability', and suggests an area

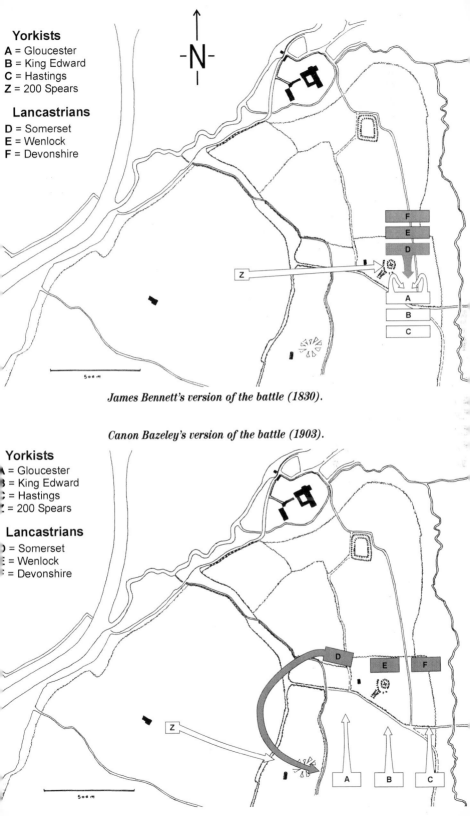

Yorkists

A = Gloucester
B = King Edward
C = Hastings
Z = 200 Spears

Lancastrians

D = Somerset
E = Wenlock
F = Devonshire

James Bennett's version of the battle (1830).

Canon Bazeley's version of the battle (1903).

Yorkists

A = Gloucester
B = King Edward
C = Hastings
Z = 200 Spears

Lancastrians

D = Somerset
E = Wenlock
F = Devonshire

near Gupshill, somewhat to the south of the Gaston. The Gaston was seen as an area which the Lancastrians retreated through rather than defended.

His version of the battle has the three 'lines' of each army behind each other rather than alongside, so making Somerset and Gloucester bear the brunt of the battle, and putting Devonshire and Hastings in the reserve. In the conduct of the battle, Holinshed is quoted extensively. After the first assault by Gloucester, Edward ordered Gloucester to withdraw. Believing this to be a retreat, the impetuous Somerset led his men from their defences only to be hit by a counter-attack from Gloucester and the unexpected charge of the 200 spears. Mad with passion, Somerset turned on Wenlock, reviled him as a traitor and killed him in the field. This was followed by a general rout. The sites referred to by Bennett and the general conduct of the aftermath of the battle differ little between Bennett and any subsequent commentator. Almost alone, though, Bennett records an estimate of the dead:

'It is computed, by some historians, that the Lancastrians lost four thousand men in this battle, but others estimate the number at only three thousand, and some much lower. Trussell, who is considered by Malone to be correct in such matters, states the exact number to be three thousand and thirty-two.'

Today, commentators shy away from this question. With no certainty of the size of the armies, the number of dead is a very open question, though 3,000 appears much too high, both because of the proportion of the army it would represent and because so many dead would leave much greater evidence of burials than we have in Tewkesbury.

The next significant account of the battle was published in 1903 in the Transactions of the Bristol and Gloucestershire Archaeological Society (BGAS). The author was Canon W. Bazeley, who was chairman of the Society. This account follows the text of the *Arrivall*. The Lancastrians are placed in the Gaston, the Yorkist line is suggested to be along the modern line of the drive to Southwick Park. The hillock in Southwick Park is identified for Somerset's charge and Tewkesbury Park for the 200 spears. The account is the first to propose the battlefield close to that now suggested by English Heritage in the Battlefield Register. Bazeley's account attempts to identify the road system south of Tewkesbury, as have all subsequent commentators. This is not an easy task and undoubtedly some roads have been omitted. The difficulty is that modern concepts of roads, lanes and paths are clear, while such distinctions were blurred 500 years ago.

In his book *The Battlefields of Britain*, published in 1950, Lieutenant Colonel Alfred Burne described Tewkesbury, concluding that Bazeley's version of events fitted the facts and the landscape. For this he earned a rebuke from the next major commentator, Lieutenant Colonel J. D. Blythe.

Writing in the BGAS transactions for 1961, Blythe made an entirely different interpretation, and was contemptuous of the Bazeley account, which he considered to be flawed in its topography. Blythe takes the *Arrivall* as his text to interpret the battle, and provides a useful commentary on the value of the Tudor chroniclers. Blythe considers the archaeological evidence and the potential to use Holm Castle as part of the Lancastrian defensive line. On the evidence of Leland's description he rejects Bennett's positioning of

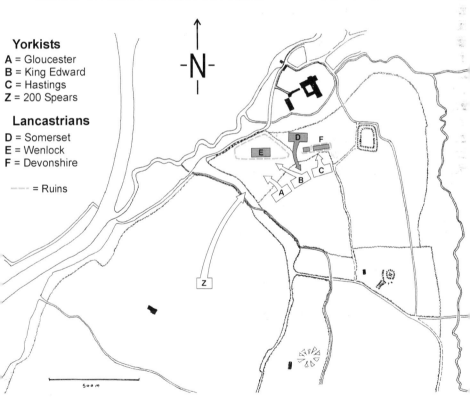

Yorkists
A = Gloucester
B = King Edward
C = Hastings
Z = 200 Spears

Lancastrians
D = Somerset
E = Wenlock
F = Devonshire

---- = Ruins

-N-

Lieutenant Colonel Blythe's version of the battle (1950).

151

Holm Castle in the Vineyards and places it on Windmill, or Holm, Hill. This we now know to have been the site of a substantial manor house, abandoned over a hundred years before the battle. With the image of a castle in his mind he speculates on a keep and curtain wall. He quotes an old man he spoke to in 1933 who told him that there used to be 'some sort of fort' on the hill. He probed the ground with an iron bar and he studied marks in the ground. Most of his hypothesis about the site has been confirmed by excavation, with the exception of the curtain wall extending 300 hundred yards to the west of the road and the bailey commanding the Vineyard slopes. No evidence for any of this has been found.

Blythe's version of the battle has the Lancastrians defending the ruins of the castle, on the assumption that remains described by Leland in 1540 as 'some ruins of the bottoms of walls' would have been substantial enough to defend seventy years earlier. He suggests that Somerset's, and possibly Wenlock's, divisions were held in reserve in Lower Lode Lane. The Yorkist attack was from the Gaston, a lane running along the northern boundary halting their progress. Somerset attacked the Yorkists, charging through the gap between the two parts of the castle fortifications. Somerset is driven along the outside of the castle fortifications to the Bloody Meadow, where he was further oppressed by the charge of the 200 spears.

Blythe's account is well argued and well considered. It suffers from the assumptions he has made about Holm Castle, now known to be wrong, and his reliance on hearsay from old men about the discovery of artefacts. Tewkesbury abounds with such stories and even where artefacts can be produced, they are almost invariably unrelated to the battle. If he had had access to later research, it seems very unlikely that Lieutenant Colonel Blythe would have reached the same conclusions.

In 1971 a booklet about the battle of Tewkesbury was published to commemorate the 500th anniversary of the battle. The authors were Messers Hammond, Shearring and Wheeler. It contains an account of the battle following the Bazeley line, setting the armies on either side of Gupshill. The Gaston is not thought to be a significant site in the battle and its location is misplaced on the plans, a mistake copied by other, later, writers. The progress of the battle is described as being very straightforward, with Somerset's charge being a general charge of his division of the army down the hill towards Gloucester. This charge was misdirected because of the nature of the ground and hit the junction of Gloucester's and the King's divisions.

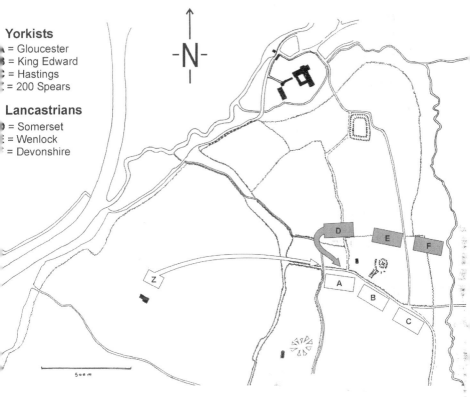

Peter Hammond's version of the battle (1971).

There is no other explanation of the hill which Somerset reached and charged down. The account glosses over these points, which are today heavily debated and considered critical to understanding the battle.

Peter Hammond's *The Battles of Barnet and Tewkesbury*, a very thorough account of the whole of the Lancastrian campaign of 1471, provides the same interpretation as his 1971 booklet. The route of the road from Tredington has been changed and follows the generally accepted route along the Swilgate valley rather than along the ridge occupied by the present road. No significance is given to the Gaston in the battle or to the hill in Somerset's charge. Hammond acknowledges that others have identified the hill as that by Southwick Park but considers that the difficulties faced by Somerset in reaching this hill, with a likely Yorkist observation post on the high ground of Stonehill, rule it out as a feasible option. This point is well made and there are numerous other practical points leading to doubt

153

about the movement described. The only wholly contemporary account, relied on by every commentator, describes Somerset's 'fellowship' departing the field, passing a lane and coming into a fair place, or close, and from the hill that was in one of the closes set fiercely upon the end of the king's 'battle'. This episode is one of the best described in the whole account. It does not describe a forward charge from the defensive lines, down the gentle slope from the hedges of the Gaston to the bottom of the shallow valley and then up the gentle slope to the higher ground beyond Gupshill. Interpretation requires a view of the purpose of Somerset's charge. If it were an impetuous movement by a commander who has no tactical plan, then a charge to still the guns or to directly target King Edward are possible explanations. Somerset was a soldier bred in a time of conflict. He had served in the army of the Duke of Burgundy, so was not a military novice. It seems inconceivable that he would not have had a tactical plan and that this move was not part of it. He would be well aware that he could not win from behind hedges and that waiting for Jasper Tudor to bring reinforcements over the Severn to sway the battle was futile. The description is clear about the hill, if not about other points. There are only two accessible hills: the hillock in Southwick Park and the slopes of the Tewkesbury Park. Either could be reached from the generally acknowledged Lancastrian lines. Each would require a different disposition of the Yorkist lines. There is not enough evidence to reach a firm conclusion. Any explanation has serious practical problems and has to be based on the balance of probability (or improbability).

In 1994, English Heritage commissioned a report on the battlefield of Tewkesbury as part of its Battlefields Register project. Arising from this, the battlefield was added to the register, providing some protection against development. The report identifies Gaston correctly and places the Lancastrians within and alongside it. The disposition of the armies is very much as earlier writers, except that Somerset is shown facing west, somewhat disconnected from Gloucester. Somerset's move is shown as being into Tewkesbury Park and down the slopes into Gloucester's flank. The *Arrivall* description of Somerset setting upon the end of the king's battle is taken literally in most interpretations, which try to position the attack into the area between Edward's and Gloucester's divisions, effectively precluding surprise. It is argued by some that any reference to the king's battle is a reference to the whole army rather than that part in his immediate command. This allows much wider

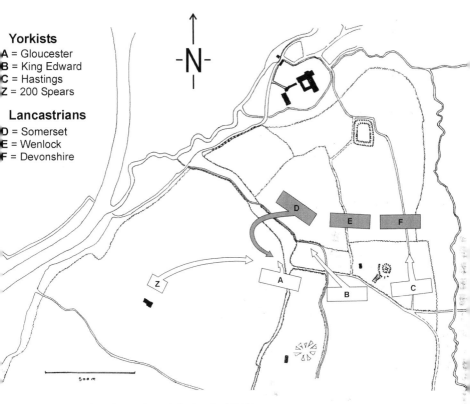

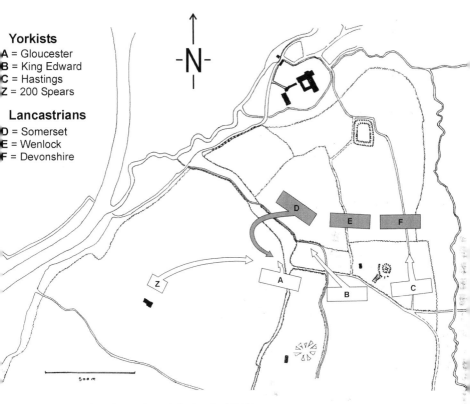

Yorkists

A = Gloucester
B = King Edward
C = Hastings
Z = 200 Spears

Lancastrians

D = Somerset
E = Wenlock
F = Devonshire

-N-

500 m

English Heritage's version of the battle (1994).

interpretation. The version of events has, inevitably, some practical problems to overcome such as charging through hedges and raises a question as to why the 200 spears, concealed in the trees on the same hill, did not ambush the Lancastrians.

The position of the battlefield on the southern edge of the town has meant that there has been considerable development within it. As late as 1975 there were major developments within the battlefield area, including the Borough Council's own offices, with little opposition and certainly no major challenge. By the time of the proposed Local Plan of 1990 the situation had changed. There were proposals to develop large tracts of land and at the public inquiry the interested parties commissioned expert reports in respect of the proposed development of the land to the east of the Gloucester Road, known as Stonehills, now a residential estate. Detailed analyses of the battle and the battle landscape were prepared by Wessex Archaeology and the Oxford Archaeology Unit. In 1998 an application to develop the two remaining Gaston fields was also the subject of a public inquiry and further analyses were produced. As most of the analysis was written to support a pre-determined position it cannot be viewed as impartial and following scientific method. It did, though, bring together all the known information pertaining to the battle and through the presentation of evidence and the cross-examination process the theories were well tested. The verdict of the inspector was that the most likely location of the initial lines of the armies was the southern one, in the vicinity of Gupshill.

Commentators have queried the Lancastrian choice of site. As well as Holm Hill, proposed by Blythe, there are two other sites which appear to be better than the Gaston field. These are the dominant hill of Tewkesbury Park, and the Mythe Tute, a hill north of Tewkesbury, at the confluence of the Severn and Avon rivers. Tewkesbury Park does seem to have many advantages, being a very dominant feature of the landscape and it must have been considered. Its disadvantage seems to be that it is easily approachable from any side, which would make it difficult to prepare defences, and the possibility of being outflanked, as the Scots were to be at Flodden, would be a real concern. To reach the Mythe Tute would mean marching through Tewkesbury and crossing the long bridge and causeway over the River Avon and its flood plain. This manoeuvre would leave the army very exposed. If attaining the Mythe were a practical possibility, then the Lancastrians would undoubtedly have done it, not to fight but to ensure their escape to Upton-upon-Severn, with its bridge and the possibility of joining with Jasper Tudor.

Though there are projects at other battlefields aimed at using science and archaeology to pinpoint features described in records, there seems no likelihood of such techniques revealing a great deal about Tewkesbury. The disagreement about the location of the battle is only over a few hundred yards. None of the interpretations can satisfactorily explain Somerset's attack as described in the *Arrivall*. We are assuming the truth of the written record, particularly as it is acknowledged to be contemporary. If the author misreported events, and in the matter of Somerset's charge there is only one source from which all others have been copied, then all the interpretations of events will be wrong. The only statements that can be made with any certainty about Tewkesbury are that there was a battle south of the town which King Edward won and once the final retribution was over the Lancastrian leadership was dead and their claim to the throne extinguished.

Acknowledgements

I should like to thank the following for their help and support:

My family, Gill, John and Sara, who between them are responsible for spotting glaring mistakes at the last moment and for producing excellent drawings and graphics on demand and always at short notice.

Everyone who agreed, with no arm twisting, to read and comment on endless drafts, particularly Margaret Pither, Peter Williams, Amanda Thomas, Elaine Davies, Bernie Willoughby, Clive Montellier and Brian Howgate.

Graham Turner for allowing his painting of the battle to adorn the cover, Adrian Fray for his information about Lord Wenlock and the portrait of Queen Margaret, Bristol and Gloucestershire Archaeological Society for access to their transactions, Tewkesbury Abbey for help with all sorts of things, Toby Clempson and John Dixon, who followed up my local history queries so willingly.

What I know about the battle is the result of many walks around the site, debates and discussions in many, and varied settings and much correspondence with historians, military historians, re-enactors and others who have all helped me piece together my story. *Thank you all.*

Index